I0411197

Table of Contents

List of Figures

List of Tables

1.0 Executive Summary

Unmanned systems are proving to have a significant impact on warfare worldwide. The true value of these systems is not to provide a direct human replacement, but rather to extend and complement human capability in a number of ways. These systems extend human reach by providing potentially unlimited persistent capabilities without degradation due to fatigue or lack of attention. Unmanned systems offer the warfighter more options and flexibility to access hazardous environments, work at small scales, or react at speeds and scales beyond human capability. With proper design of bounded autonomous capabilities, unmanned systems can also reduce the high cognitive load currently placed on operators/supervisors. Moreover, increased autonomy can enable humans to delegate those tasks that are more effectively done by computer, including synchronizing activities between multiple unmanned systems, software agents and warfighters—thus freeing humans to focus on more complex decision making.

While the potential of autonomy is great, there have been many obstacles to general broad acceptance of unmanned systems, and, specifically, the autonomous capabilities needed to realize the benefits of autonomy in military applications. Most Department of Defense (DoD) deployments of unmanned systems have been motivated by the pressing needs of conflict, particularly the threat of improvised explosive devices and the need for persistent intelligence, surveillance and reconnaissance (ISR) data collection. To date, most of the demonstrated benefits of autonomous systems have been in air or ground applications, but there exists no reason that they could not be effective in maritime and space missions as well.

The Task Force was charged to assist the DoD in understanding and preparing to take maximum practical advantage of advances in autonomy by reviewing relevant technologies, ongoing research and the current autonomy-relevant plans of the Military Services. The Department asked the Task Force to identify new opportunities to more aggressively use autonomy in military missions, to anticipate vulnerabilities and to make recommendations for overcoming operational difficulties and systemic barriers to realizing the full potential of autonomous systems.

1.1. Misperceptions about Autonomy are Limiting its Adoption

Autonomy is a capability (or a set of capabilities) that enables a particular action of a system to be automatic or, within programmed boundaries, "self-governing." Unfortunately, the word "autonomy" often conjures images in the press and the minds of some military leaders of computers making independent decisions and taking uncontrolled action. While the reality of what autonomy is and can do is quite different from those conjured images, these concerns are—in some cases—limiting its adoption. It should be made clear that all autonomous systems are *supervised* by human operators at some level, and autonomous systems' software embodies the designed limits on the actions and decisions delegated to the computer. Instead of viewing autonomy as an intrinsic property of an unmanned vehicle in isolation, the design and operation of autonomous systems needs to be considered in terms of *human-system collaboration.*

Due to software complexity, autonomous systems present a variety of challenges to commanders, operators and developers, both in how these systems interact in dynamic environments and in human-system collaboration. For commanders, a key challenge presented by the complexity of software is that the design space and tradeoffs for incorporating autonomy into a mission are not well understood and can result in unintended operational consequences. A key challenge for operators is maintaining the human-machine collaboration needed to execute their mission, which is frequently handicapped by poor design. A key challenge facing unmanned system developers is the move from a hardware-oriented, vehicle-centric development and acquisition process to one that addresses the primacy of software in creating autonomy. For commanders and operators in particular, these challenges can collectively be characterized as a *lack of trust* that the autonomous functions of a given system will operate as intended in all situations.

In addition to software challenges, the urgent deployment of unmanned systems to theater left little time to refine concepts of operation (CONOPS) which, when coupled with the lack of assets and time to support pre-deployment exercises, created operational challenges. Consequently, operational forces often first learned to use autonomous systems in combat. As a result, many systems were used in ways not anticipated by developers, and additional staff was required to work around limitations in system capabilities. Moving forward, it is important that this operational experience is communicated to the development community so that lessons in the field can ultimately influence upgrades to existing systems and the designs of future systems.

To address the issues that are limiting the more extensive use of autonomy, the Task Force recommends a crosscutting approach which includes the following key elements (elaborated in the body of the report and the sections of the executive summary as indicated):

- **The DoD should abandon the debate over definitions of levels of autonomy and embrace a three-facet (cognitive echelon, mission timelines, human-machine system trade spaces) autonomous systems framework (Section 1.2).** This framework would assist program managers in shaping technology programs, as well as assist acquisition officers and developers in making key decisions for the design and evaluation of future systems. It would also aid commanders and operators in visualizing the scope and impact of a particular autonomous capability. The details of this important framework are discussed further in the following section.
- **The Assistant Secretary of Defense for Research and Engineering (ASD(R&E)) should work with the Military Services to establish a coordinated science and technology (S&T) program guided by feedback from operational experience and evolving mission requirements (Section 1.3).** This program should especially leverage feedback from the operators who have used unmanned systems in the recent conflicts.

■ **The Military Services should structure autonomous systems acquisition programs to separate the autonomy software from the vehicle platform. Further, they should initiate at least one open software design project, preferably for an existing platform, that decouples autonomy from the vehicle and deploys proven technology to reduce manpower, increase capability and adapt to future missions (Section 1.4.1).** Because the critical capabilities provided by autonomy are embedded in software and the traditional DoD acquisition milestones are dominated by hardware considerations, new acquisition techniques are needed.

■ **The Under Secretary of Defense for Acquisition, Technology and Logistics (USD(AT&L)) should create developmental and operational test and evaluation (T&E) techniques that focus on the unique challenges of autonomy (Section 1.4.2).** DoD needs new technology to assist the test community with certifying systems at the end of development—a situation that has not yet happened because currently fielded autonomy technologies have by-passed the formal test process due to the pressing demands of the recent conflicts.

■ **The Services should include the lessons learned from using autonomous systems in the recent conflicts into professional military education, war games, exercises and operational training (Section 1.4.3).** These actions will help remedy some of the operational challenges associated with unmanned systems that resulted from the fact that the demands of conflict forced the deployment of prototype and developmental capability before the operational forces were fully prepared to receive them.

■ **The Defense Intelligence Agency (DIA) and the Intelligence Community should track adversarial capabilities with autonomous systems and the Services should aggressively include these threats in war games, training, simulations and exercises (Section 1.5).** This will reduce capability surprise, speed innovation of DoD capabilities and provide opportunities for high-fidelity testing and evaluation.

The remainder of this Executive Summary provides a more detailed description of the recommendations, and is organized by the following topics: technical challenges; acquisition, development and transition issues; test and evaluation; and avoiding capability surprise.

1.2. Create an Autonomous Systems Reference Framework to Replace "Levels of Autonomy"

During the design of an autonomous system, a significant number of decisions are made to allocate specific cognitive functions to either the computer or the human operator. These decisions reflect system-level trade-offs between performance factors, such as computationally efficient, optimal solutions for expected scenarios versus susceptibility to failures or the need for increased manpower when variations in the scenarios or new situations occur. In many cases, these design decisions have been made implicitly without an examination of the consequences to the ultimate system users or to overall acquisition, maintenance, or manpower costs.

The Task Force reviewed many of the DoD-funded studies on "levels of autonomy" and concluded that they are not particularly helpful to the autonomy design process. These studies attempt to aid the development process by defining taxonomies and grouping functions needed for generalized scenarios. They are counter-productive because they focus too much attention on the computer rather than on the *collaboration* between the computer and its operator/supervisor to achieve the desired capabilities and effects. Further, these taxonomies imply that there are discrete levels of intelligence for autonomous systems, and that classes of vehicle systems can be designed to operate at a specific level for the entire mission.

These taxonomies are misleading both from a cognitive science perspective and from observations of actual practice. Cognitively, system autonomy is a continuum from complete human control of all decisions to situations where many functions are delegated to the computer with only high-level supervision and/or oversight from its operator. Multiple concurrent functions may be needed to evince a desired capability, and subsets of functions may require a human in the loop, while other functions can be delegated at the same time. Thus, at any stage of a mission, it is possible for a system to be in more than one discrete level simultaneously. In practice, treating "levels of autonomy" as a developmental roadmap has created a focus on machines, rather than on the human-machine system. This has led to designs that provide specific functions rather than overall resilient capability.

The Task Force recommends that the DoD abandon the use of "levels of autonomy" and replace them with an autonomous systems reference framework that explicitly:

- **Focuses design decisions on the explicit allocation of cognitive functions and responsibilities between the human and computer to achieve specific capabilities,**
- **Recognizes that these allocations may vary by mission phase as well as echelon and**
- **Makes the high-level system trades inherent in the design of autonomous capabilities visible.**

A Task Force-developed candidate reference framework is presented in Figure 1-1 to illustrate the concept and provide the Department with a point of departure for efforts to refine and adopt this structure across all DoD autonomous systems programs. While the framework will be described in detail in Chapter 3, "Technical Challenges of Autonomy," the framework captures the three classes of design decisions for autonomy that meet the above criteria and provides the visibility to ensure that they are addressed explicitly during the requirements specification, design and review/approval phases of the acquisition process. A design should be examined from each of these three views:

- The **cognitive echelon view** in which increases in the autonomy of component agents and roles also increases the importance of coordination across echelons and roles as joint activity unfolds,

- The **mission dynamics view** in which autonomy may be employed in different ways for various mission phases and effects how different agents synchronize activities across mission phases, roles, and echelons as new events, disruptions, and opportunities arise,
- The **complex system trades space view** in which design choices about where and how to inject autonomy changes how the larger system balances multiple performance trade-offs; the risk is that autonomy related improvements in one area can produce unintended negative consequences in other aspects of total system performance.

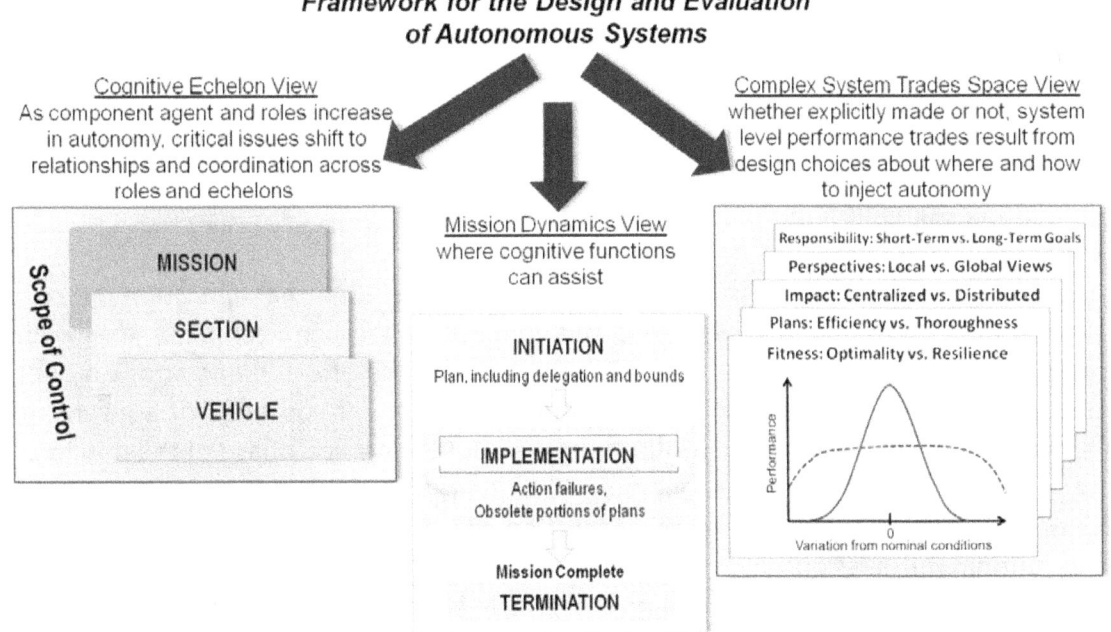

Figure 1-1 Framework for the Design and Evaluation of Autonomous Systems

The *cognitive echelon view,* expanded in Figure 1-2 below, considers how autonomy supports the scope of control for canonical types of "users," extends their reach into theater and facilitates adapting to surprises. The vehicle/sensor operator controls vehicle movement, sensor operation, communications and status monitoring. The section/team leader has responsibility for mission planning and re-planning as well as multi-agent (vehicle) collaboration. The scope of control for the mission commander/executive officer includes scenario assessment and understanding, scenario planning and decision making and contingency management. There is extensive communication and coordination among these operators, and each cognitive function can be allocated to or shared between the computer or the operator/supervisor.

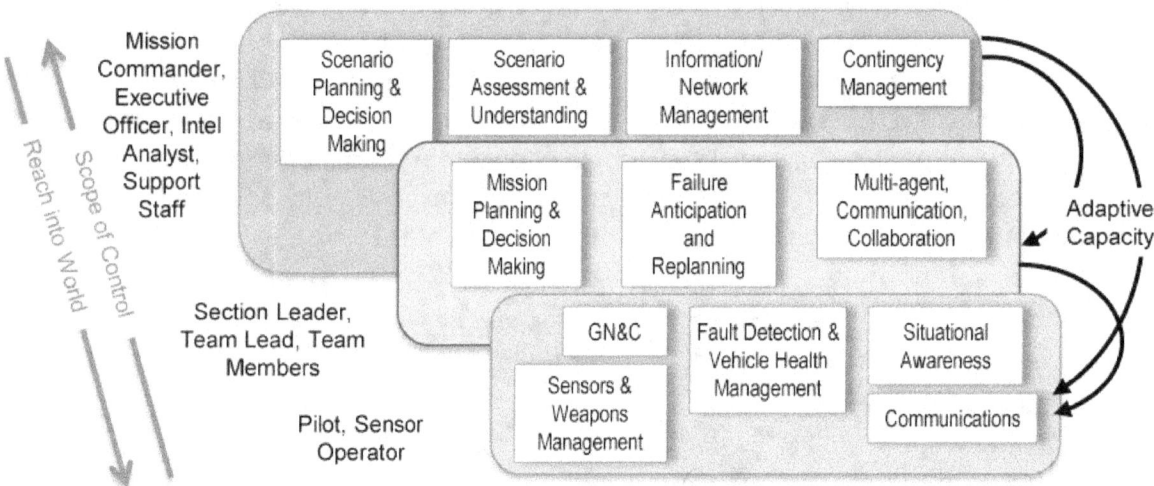

Figure 1-2 Autonomous System Reference Framework - Scope of Cognitive Functions Across Echelons

The *mission dynamics view* of the framework recognizes that the allocation of cognitive functions may vary over the course of a mission based on such factors as environmental complexity and required response time. To date, most of the effort in acquiring and applying autonomy appears to be for the implementation of the nominal portions of a given mission, such as navigation within a planned profile over the implementation phase of the mission.

Increased autonomy can assist with the adaptation of any aspect of a plan that might require changes during the mission, such as new targets, goals, additional information, degraded weather or vehicle performance conditions, etc. The initiation phase and termination phases also present opportunities to incorporate autonomy to reduce manpower and improve efficiency.

The *complex system trades space view* of the framework is summarized in Table 1-1, below, and reflects the five key system-level trades that often dominate performance after the system is deployed. (These trades will be described in further detail in Chapter 3 and will be accompanied by a detailed example taken from the use of Predators.) These system trades are made in all designs, either explicitly or implicitly, and the Task Force recommends that they be an explicit part of the requirements, design and review process. System trades made without explicit awareness of their respective implications can lead to many unintended consequences, including higher manpower and training costs, avoidable collateral damage, failures attributed to "human error" and underutilization.

Table 1-1 The Complex System Trades Space View

Trade Space	Trades	Benefits	Unintended Consequences
Fitness	Optimality vs. Resilience	More precise results for understood situations	Increased brittleness
Plans	Efficiency vs. Thoroughness	Balanced use of computational resources	Locked into wrong plan/difficulty revising plan
Impact	Centralized vs. Distributed	Ability to tailor actions to appropriate echelon	High cost of coordination
Perspectives	Local vs. Global Views	Ability to balance scale/area of action with resolution	Data overload; reduced speed of decision making
Responsibility	Short-Term vs. Long-Term goals	Builds trust tailoring risk management to goals, priorities, context	Break down in collaboration and coordination

1.3. Technical Challenges Remain, Some Proven Autonomy Capability Underutilized

The cognitive echelons in Figure 1-1 show that autonomous capabilities can provide value throughout the command structure, not just for vehicle or platform control. At higher echelons, artificial intelligence (AI) can autonomously fuse and abstract data, as well as manage, prioritize and route data provided by unmanned vehicles. Likewise, the data can be used to autonomously produce plans, anticipate failures and manage coordination with other members in net-centric warfare. The Task Force reviewed the state of the art in AI and other related autonomy technologies as well as those that are currently in practice. Based on the Task Force's observations, we have concluded that existing, proven autonomous capabilities are underutilized. Moreover, existing Department research and development (R&D) is not aggressively pursuing fundamental capabilities that would increase performance at all echelons.

To date, the most extensive use of autonomy has been at the lower echelon of vehicle/platform scope of control. However, even at the lower level, applications have not taken full advantage of proven autonomous capabilities in automated take-off and landing, waypoint navigation, automatic return to base upon loss of communications and path planning. The current use of autonomy has been inconsistent across platforms.

As noted earlier, autonomy has been added without explicitly considering the consequences and trade-offs on the overall system. New autonomous technologies can have a dramatic impact on capacity and performance of specific parts of a system. Current designs of autonomous systems, and current design methods for increasing autonomy, can create **brittle** platforms, and have led to missed opportunities and new system failure modes when new capabilities are deployed.[1] An example of the former is the unsustainable operating costs, in terms of increases in manpower and training, which have been required to make use of new capabilities in challenging missions. An example of the latter includes new failure paths associated with more autonomous platforms, which has been seen in friendly fire fatalities.[2,3] Brittle autonomous technologies result in unintended consequences and unnecessary performance trade-offs, and this brittleness, which is resident in many current designs, has severely retarded the potential benefits that could be obtained by using advances in autonomy.

With proper designs that consider each of the three system views in Figure 1-1,[4] currently-available autonomy technology should not only support individual vehicle autonomy with less manpower, but it should also meet the goal of providing an individual with the ability to operate multiple platforms for many types of missions, or at least significant phases of missions. With impending budget pressures on the Department, the Task Force believes that these manpower efficiencies may be an important benefit of increasing autonomy in unmanned systems.

Chapter 3 will review the status of technology enablers required to provide autonomous mission capability at the cognitive echelons and throughout all phases of a mission as defined in the reference framework. In addition to the inconsistent use of navigational autonomous capabilities, the Task Force believes that autonomy technologies (Figure 1-3, highlighted in orange) have been well proven in laboratory and research settings but remain underutilized for vehicle fault detection and health management, communications management, mission planning and decision support, as well in contingency planning for responses to off-nominal conditions.

The study also identified cognitive functions (Figure 1-3, highlighted in red) in which beneficial technology is not yet mature enough to support an operator confidently delegating to the computer. To address these shortfalls, **the Task Force recommends that ASD(R&E) work with the Military Services to create a coordinated S&T program to strengthen key enabling autonomy technologies (perceptual processing, planning, learning, human-robot interaction, natural language understanding and multi-agent coordination)** with emphasis on:

- Natural user interfaces and trusted human-system collaboration.
- Perception and situational awareness to operate in a complex battle space.
- Large-scale teaming of manned and unmanned systems.

---

[1] Woods, D.D. and E. Hollnagel. 2006. Joint Cognitive Systems: Patterns in Cognitive Systems Engineering. Boca Raton, FL: Taylor & Francis.

[2] Herz, Robert. 2010. Human Factors Issues in Combat Identification.

[3] Hawley, John K. and Anna L. Mares. 2012. Human Performance Challenges for the Future Force: Lessons from Patriot after the Second Gulf War.

[4] Zieba, S., P. Polet, and F. Vanderhaegen. 2011. Using Adjustable Autonomy and Human–Machine Cooperation to Make a Human–Machine System Resilient-Application to a Ground Robotic System. Information Sciences 181(3): 379–397.

■ Test and evaluation of autonomous systems.

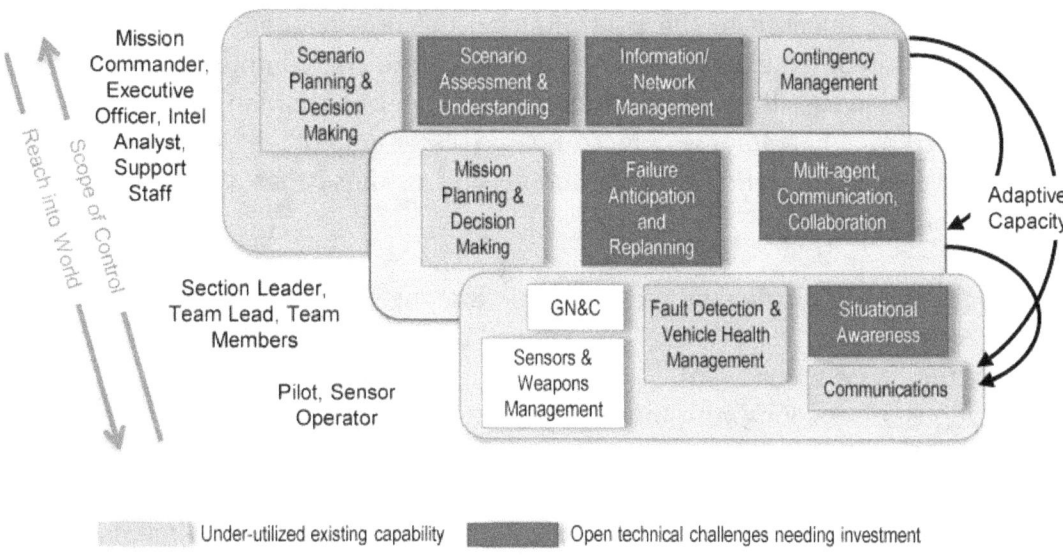

Figure 1-3 Status of Technology Deployment and Remaining Challenges

More detail on the recommended research program is provided in Chapter 3.

The Task Force noted, with admiration, the ingenuity of the deployed forces as they adapted autonomous, unmanned systems to the needs of combat. Often, these systems were used in ways that were not anticipated by the requirements process or by the engineers who designed the systems.   It is important to continue to achieve the benefits of experimentation in operational conditions, but the Department must ensure that lessons learned from this experience influence both the development of technical capability and the design of future autonomous systems. **The Task Force recommends that the Department's S&T program be stimulated by realistic challenge problems that are motivated by operational experience and evolving mission needs. To ensure that the technologists and designers get direct feedback from the operators, ASD(R&E) and the Military Services should schedule periodic, on-site collaborations that bring together academia, government and not-for-profit labs and industry and military operators to focus on appropriate challenge problems.**

The development and acquisition of autonomous systems requires new technical capability, particularly in the design and testing of complex software systems, beyond that required by most other weapons. **The Task Force also recommends that the Department and the Services strengthen the government's technical workforce for autonomy by attracting AI and software engineering experts and establishing career paths and promotion opportunities to ensure their retention.**

1.4. Autonomous Systems Pose Unique Acquisition Challenges

Because autonomous systems provide a new capability with which operational experience is lacking, the DoD requirements definition and acquisition processes have been difficult. No unmanned, autonomous systems have formally completed operational test and evaluation (OT&E) prior to being released to the field. Rather, the urgent needs of combat forced the deployment of prototype or developmental systems before the completion of all acquisition milestones. The problems with the DoD requirements and acquisition processes have been extensively studied by other Defense Science Board (DSB) Task Forces;[5] therefore, the current Task Force limited its investigation of acquisition issues to those that are uniquely associated with autonomous systems.

1.4.1. Autonomous systems development requires increased focus on software

Unlike many other defense systems, the critical capabilities provided by autonomy are embedded in the system software. However, the traditional acquisition milestones for unmanned systems, often along with the focus of the development contractor, are dominated by hardware considerations. Autonomy software is frequently treated as an afterthought or assumed to be a component that can be added to the platform at a later date—independent of sensors, processing power, communications and other elements that may limit computational intelligence.

To address this situation with developers, an autonomy reference framework, based on that presented in Figure 1-1, should be used throughout the requirements definition and design phases of autonomous systems development programs. This will ensure that software issues do not get lost within a hardware-oriented, vehicle-centric acquisition process. Specifically, software should be designed with an open architecture structure to facilitate modification to adapt to evolving requirements and to add new capabilities after the platform has been deployed.

The Task Force recommends that the Military Services structure autonomous systems acquisition programs to separate the autonomy software from the vehicle platform. The autonomy program should create a government-owned software package, with an open architecture, that is designed with published interfaces to enable modifications and expansion by any contactor, laboratory or government agency without having to go back to the original developer. This package can be provided as government-furnished equipment to the platform developer. The Task Force has seen several initiatives (see Chapter 4) across the DoD and the Military Services that provide examples consistent with this recommendation. At a minimum, if an autonomous system is acquired with a single integrated hardware/software procurement, the government program manager should structure the contract to acquire full government

---

[5] DSB Task Force on Improvements to Services Contracting, March 2011; DSB Task Force on Fulfillment of Urgent Operational Needs, July 2009; DSB Task Force on Creating a DoD Strategic Acquisition Platform, April 2009; and DSB Task Force on Department of Defense Policies and Procedures for the Acquisition of Information Technology, March 2009.

ownership of the autonomy software, including source code and all documentation required to enable a third party upgrade to the functional capability.

Most of the unmanned systems currently in the DoD inventory consist of contractor-proprietary, on-board autonomy and control software, with often closed, proprietary operator control systems (OCS). Under such circumstances, the government is constrained to returning to the development contractor for all enhancements, often slowing the pace of innovation and evolution of operational capability. There are many efforts underway to create common OCSs able to manage more than one class of autonomous system. For example, the Army is developing a single OCS that will be capable of controlling all of its small unmanned aerial vehicles.

The ability to upgrade autonomy software without creating new platforms is key in both reducing manpower and in being able to address new, evolving missions with the existing inventory of unmanned vehicles. To increase the Department's flexibility in dealing with this future environment, **the Task Force recommends that each Military Service initiate at least one open software design project, preferably for an existing platform, that decouples autonomy from the vehicle and deploys proven technology to reduce manpower, increase capability and adapt to future missions.** While such initiatives may require negotiations with the existing platform prime-contractors to gain government control of proprietary software, these investments will likely pay off in the long run.

In addition to the acquisition challenges associated with embedded software, significant attention must be directed at protecting this software from cyber threats during both development/acquisition and operations. While the Task Force recognizes the importance of addressing cyber security issues, we did not have the resources for a thorough examination of this issue.

1.4.2. Test and evaluation (T&E) of autonomous systems requires a new view and new technology

The reference framework in Figure 1-1 and the trade spaces described in Table 1-1 provide a significant re-conceptualization of how the software underlying autonomous platforms should be tested. This is true both in terms of protocols used for development and operational testing and in the infrastructure needed to capture the nature and scale of the interactions between subsystems and between the software and the human. The fact that autonomy software interacts with a dynamic environment in a non-deterministic manner is particularly challenging, especially for agencies that are used to full-path regression testing that validates every individual requirement. The reference framework highlights the need to confirm how the autonomous system provides its operator and upper echelons of direct and indirect users with the basis for making the decisions delegated to it during different mission phases. It also highlights the need for measures and models of the dimensions of system resilience/brittleness that can be used early in systems development as well as later in T&E. The new T&E capabilities foreseen by the Task Force will need to take into account the system wide reverberations of increases in autonomy as captured in the reference framework. The T&E capabilities include: testing the ability to coordinate, across roles and echelons, with autonomous capabilities; testing the ability to synchronize and adapt as missions unfold in time; and testing the ability to reduce the risk of unintended negative consequences that counteract local benefits of localized injections of autonomy by detecting the warning signs of system level deficiencies such as brittleness and data overload.

The Task Force recommends that USD(AT&L) establish a research program to create the technologies needed for developmental and operational T&E that address the unique challenges of autonomy. Among the topics that this research should address are:

- Techniques for defining test cases and expected results that overcome the difficulty of enumerating all conditions and non-deterministic responses that autonomy will generate in response to complex environments,
- Methods and metrics for confirming that an autonomous system will perform or interact with its human supervisor as intended and for measuring the user's trust in the system,
- Interfaces that make the basis of autonomous system decisions more apparent to its users,
- Test environments that include direct and indirect users at all echelons, as appropriate for an intended capability and
- Robust simulation to create meaningful test environments.

Based on the results of this research, it is likely that the Department will need to improve its operational test ranges so that they can better support the evaluation of autonomous systems.

1.4.3. Transition of autonomous systems to the field requires better preparation
Because the demands of conflict forced the deployment of prototype and developmental capability, the Military Services were unprepared for unmanned, autonomous systems at many levels. Manning concepts were not in place, spare parts were often unavailable and sparing, logistics support and maintenance needs were unknown. The connectivity and bandwidth required to handle the enormous volumes of data collected by unmanned platforms, as well as the capability to process and distribute this information to all who needed it, were not available. (Processing and exploitation of large volumes of ISR data is itself an application that will benefit from autonomy technology.) Additionally, the CONOPS and associated training were immature, thus preventing the troops from using everything provided them and hampering their ability to use what they had as effectively as they might otherwise have. The lack of preparedness for unmanned systems persisted through the conflicts in Iraq and Afghanistan, as usage evolved through operational experimentation in unimagined ways as illustrated by the significant impact of enabling the projection of force through arming Predator UAVs

None of this is surprising, or particularly unique to autonomy, since similar experience has been observed with other advanced systems that were rushed into combat. However, what it means is that, as the Department moves into a post-conflict environment, there is still a need for the Military Services to improve the understanding of the role and benefits of autonomous systems. **The Task Force recommends the following actions to achieve operational improvements in the usage of autonomy:**

- **Include sections about autonomous operations and their value in professional military education.**
- **Include unmanned, autonomous system concepts (in all domains—air, ground, maritime and space) in war games and pre-deployment operational training.**
- **Ensure that lessons learned from using unmanned systems in the current conflict are broadly disseminated and are formally reviewed by the Military Services for training and operational improvements for current systems.**
- **Develop a unified (all Military Services and domains) feedback mechanism in which operators can input experiences and recommendations on autonomous system performance and behavior during both training and mission operations so that common experiences can influence autonomous system design and human-system collaboration.**
- **Develop operational training techniques that explicitly build trust in autonomous systems and validate projected manning efficiencies.**
- **Invest in modeling and simulation capabilities required to support early operation training to influence CONOPS development, mission planning, training and logistics support.**

1.5. Avoid Capability Surprise by Anticipating Adversary Use of Autonomous Systems

The barrier to entry for using unmanned, autonomous systems is very low and the motivation is high. Research and demonstrations related to intelligent robots are common undergraduate projects in universities worldwide. The benefits of the United States' use of unmanned aerial vehicles (UAVs) to conduct surveillance in current conflicts are broadly understood. As a result, over 50 countries have purchased unmanned surveillance vehicles, and the international market for the technology is very robust.

Wide availability of unmanned systems technology, combined with potential adversaries who might be less concerned with rules of engagement and collateral damage or are capable of applying advanced software concepts already in the scientific literature, could result in a range of challenging threats. While all vehicles sizes are possible, the threats from smaller platforms, particularly small UAVs, that can be launched covertly from the ground, may be an especially difficult threat to counter--even in the presence of U.S. air superiority. Adversary applications of this technology include:

- Significant harassment on the battlefield,
- Low intensity adversary surveillance prior to transition to hostile action and
- Asymmetric attacks on the U.S. homeland.

Despite the likelihood of this threat, as discussed in Chapter 5, the Task Force found little evidence of planning to counter adversary use of autonomy and unmanned systems against the U.S. Unless this situation is addressed, adversary use of autonomous systems may be the next "knowable" capability surprise. Consequently, **the Task Force recommends that:**

- **DIA and the Intelligence Community develop threat assessments for potential adversaries that determine their posture and potential intent relative to the use of autonomous systems.**
- **The Military Services develop tactics, techniques and procedures for countering adversary use of unmanned capabilities. Specifically, include adversary use of autonomous systems in war games, simulations and exercises. Do not constrain this usage by U.S. systems or rules of engagement.**
- **The Services also establish red teams to study U.S. systems and develop adversary responses.**

In addition to explicitly preparing for adversary use of autonomous systems, greater attention should be directed at the vulnerabilities of the unmanned systems that are currently in the U.S. inventory or under development. Most experience to date has been in benign threat environments with unchallenged air superiority. Specific vulnerabilities that development program managers and operators should consider are physical threats to the platform, jamming and cyber-attacks.

2.0 Operational Benefits of Autonomy

The Task Force has observed, through briefings and site visits, that air and ground applications of autonomy, in particular, have advanced furthest technologically and are making the most significant impact across DoD operations. However, their advancement is largely due to the operational demands of war efforts over the past decade and does not necessarily portend the operational needs of future battle environments. In fact, with piracy on the rise in recent years, as well as the burgeoning presence of space applications of other nation-states, future operational demands may shift toward these spaces. Consequently, DoD must maintain a balanced approach in research, development, test and evaluation (RDT&E) investments that account for the ecology of the specific mission needs in the context of each of the operating environments.

This chapter provides a summary of the operational status of unmanned vehicle (UxV) technology in the four operational domains. More detail on the status of these domains is provided in Appendix A.

2.1. Unmanned Aerial Vehicles

While UAVs have long held great promise for military operations, the technology has only recently matured enough to exploit that potential. In recent years, the UAV mission scope has expanded from tactical reconnaissance to include most of the capabilities within the ISR and battle space awareness mission areas. Without the constraint of the nominal 12-hour limitation of a human in the cockpit, UAVs can maintain sensors and precision weapons over an area of interest at great distances for longer periods of time, providing situational awareness to all levels of command.

For example, the Air Force is now conducting Remote-Split Operations (RSO), allowing service members who are controlling aircraft in multiple locations in Continental United States (CONUS) to switch between controlling aircraft in different theaters as mission and weather requirements dictate and conduct shift changes in mid-flight. Together, these capabilities enable greater continuity and persistent visibility of the battlefield, at a third of the forward-deployed footprint compared to that of line-of-sight operations.

In addition to expanded persistence, the integration of ISR and strike on the same unmanned platform, coupled with direct connectivity of UAV operators to ground forces, has led to reduced reaction time and is saving lives of U.S. troops on the ground. Moreover, autonomous technology is increasing the safety of unmanned aircraft during auto-takeoff and landing (for those organizations leveraging that technology) and reducing workload via waypoint navigation and orbit management. In addition, due to developments in sense-and-avoid technologies, redundant flight controls, experience and revised procedures, the accident rate for most unmanned systems now mirrors manned aircraft.

Unmanned aircraft clearly have a critical role in the DoD operational future. However, the development of these systems is still in the formative stage, and challenges remain relative to training, integration of command and control and integration of UAVs into the National Air Space. For example, there is no high-fidelity training environment for UAV pilots and sensor operators today. There is no computer-based training system for Predator crews to operate in conjunction with real-world weapons tactics training. A full simulation training system is sorely needed to ensure that the level of proficiency of aerial unmanned crews is maintained. Moreover, there are vastly different approaches to training between Military Services that also need to be reconciled. For example, it takes the Air Force ten months to fully train a Predator crew member, whereas the Army only requires three months of training for that same position. More focus should be given to using autonomy technologies to enhance training. Also, integration of command and control of unmanned systems within existing and future battle command systems is not well understood. The integration of the ISR products provided to battle command systems by unmanned systems and their distribution to the warfighters are not optimal.

2.2. Unmanned Ground Systems

Similar to the value UAVs bring to the skies in the form of persistent visibility, Unmanned Ground Systems (UGVs) bring benefits to land in standoff capability. Generally designed as sensory prosthetics, weapons systems or for gaining access to areas inaccessible by humans, UGVs are reducing service member exposure to life threatening tasks by enabling them to identify and neutralize improvised explosive devices (IEDs) from a distance. Today, UGVs are largely used in support of counter-IED and route clearance operations, using robotic arms attached to, and operated by, modified Mine Resistant Ambush Protected (MRAP) vehicles and remotely controlled robotic systems. To a lesser extent, UGVs are being used in dismounted and tactical operations, providing initial and in-depth reconnaissance for soldiers and Marines.

In general, UGVs in combat operations face two primary challenges: negotiating terrain and obstacles on the battlefield and performing kinetic operations within the Rules of Engagement (ROE). Terrain negotiation and obstacle avoidance are driven by mechanical capabilities coupled with pattern recognition and problem solving skills. Operations within the ROE, however, represent a higher order, biomimetic cognitive skill that must fall within the commander's intent. Going forward, development efforts should aim to advance technologies to better overcome these challenges. Particularly in the latter case, the development of autonomous systems that allow the operator/commander to delegate specific cognitive functions, that may or may not change during the course of a mission or engagement, would appear to be an important milestone in evolution from remotely controlled robotics to autonomous systems.

The current DoD Unmanned Systems Integrated Roadmap[6] identifies four key mission areas that aim to focus development efforts on: reconnaissance and surveillance, target identification and designation, counter-mine warfare and chemical, biological, radiological, nuclear or high-

---

[6] Department of Defense. 2011. FY2011–2034 Unmanned Systems Integrated Roadmap

yield explosive (CBRNE) missions. What the roadmap seems to lack is adequate consideration of how DoD can counter enemies who use highly mobile, lethal autonomous systems that lack the higher-order cognitive capabilities to conduct combat engagements within the confines of international treaties and the laws of land warfare.

While the engagement of a robot in a non-kinetic environment may appear challenging, the development of autonomous ground combat systems to counter enemy ground combat systems is a much harder, but nevertheless realistic, scenario which the Task Force recommends DoD address as it prepares for future challenges and guards against capability surprise.

2.3. Unmanned Maritime Vehicles

Mission areas for unmanned maritime vehicles (UMVs) can generally be categorized into surface and underwater domains (unmanned surface vehicles (USVs) and unmanned underwater vehicles (UUVs), respectively). Unmanned surface vehicles "operate with near-continuous contact with the surface of the water, including conventional hull crafts, hydrofoils and semi-submersibles. Unmanned underwater vehicles are made to operate without necessary contact with the surface (but may need to be near surface for communications purposes) and some can operate covertly."[7]

USV missions may include antisubmarine warfare (ASW), maritime security, surface warfare, special operations forces support, electronic warfare and maritime interdiction operations support.[8] The Navy has identified a similarly diverse, and often overlapping, range of missions for UUVs, which include ISR, mine countermeasures, ASW, inspection/identification, oceanography, communication/navigation network node, payload delivery, information operations and time-critical strike.[9]

Driven largely by the wars in Iraq and Afghanistan—in which airpower and ISR capabilities play a pivotal role—platforms like Predator, Reaper and Global Hawk are at the forefront of the unmanned systems revolution; however, sea-based platforms offer many of the same benefits afforded by aerial systems in domains that will likely be of future strategic importance to the United States. The future importance of these vehicles is further emphasized by the recent attention and prominence assigned to the concept of Air-Sea Battle in post-Iraq/Afghanistan planning scenarios. As noted in the recently released *Unmanned Systems Integrated Roadmap FY2011-2036*, "with emerging threats such as piracy, natural resource disputes, drug trafficking and weapons proliferation, a rapid response capability is needed in all maritime regions. DoD continues to expand the range of missions supported by unmanned systems in the maritime domain."[10]

---

[7] Department of Defense. 2011. FY2011–2034 Unmanned Systems Integrated Roadmap
[8] U.S. Navy. 2007. Unmanned Surface Vehicle Master Plan.
[9] U.S. Navy. 2004. Unmanned Undersea Vehicle (UUV) Master Plan.
[10] Department of Defense. 2011. FY2011–2034 Unmanned Systems Integrated Roadmap

Not surprisingly, the primary DoD user of UMVs is the U.S. Navy, which has played a central role in the RDT&E of current UMV platforms. A key driver of the Navy's support for UMV technology is the broad range of missions to which these systems can be applied. In some instances, real-world fleet experimentation and technology demonstrations have already occurred. Mine clearing appears to be a mission particularly well-suited for the capabilities of UMVs, although there are still some challenges associated with congested waters.

Over the long-term, the Navy is looking to develop Real Time (RT) sensor processing for UUVs. Currently, a UUV will perform a mission in which it collects data, which is then transferred for processing after the vehicle has been recovered. Nevertheless, there are situations where RT or Near Real Time (NRT) data transfer is critical and must be considered in the early stages of platform design.

Each of the above focus areas acts as a driver for greater degrees of UMV autonomy – as developments in one focus area advance (or plateau), so too will the need—or opportunity—for greater autonomy. This is certainly true with regard to communications (including dynamic navigation, data processing/dissemination and command and control (C2)) in which technology cannot overcome certain physical limitations of the marine environment, essentially mandating greater autonomy. Furthermore, as improvements are made in energy density/endurance, unmanned maritime vehicles will be able to conduct far-forward missions, both enabling and capitalizing on future advances in autonomy.

2.4. Unmanned Space Systems

The role of autonomy in space systems can be organized in two categories: types of autonomous operations (mission and satellite) and degrees of autonomy (ranging from limited to full autonomy). Mission Operations refer to the ability of a satellite and/or payload to execute assigned missions without operator involvement/intervention. Satellite Operations refer to the ability of a satellite (or satellite bus) to execute routine operations to keep the systems operating in support of the payload and mission (i.e., housekeeping). A system with a limited delegation of cognitive functions is unable to execute significant sets of functionalities/tasks without substantial operator involvement/intervention, whereas a system with delegation of more complex decisions to the autonomy software is able to execute a full set of functionalities/tasks without operator involvement/intervention.

The current forecast of increasingly distributed satellite architectures may result in increases to the number and diversity of spacecraft. At the present, the Task Force is not aware of a formal Air Force initiative for autonomy. (It should be noted, however, that there are efforts to "automate" ground antenna systems, for example, the Naval Research Laboratory (NRL) cubesat ground station is completely automated. NRL operations at Blossom Point are also largely automated and have been for several years.) The 50th Space Wing's Integrated Operations Environment (IOE) and Air Force Space Command (AFSPC) Satellite Enterprise Transformation (SET) are the most significant, current modernization efforts. The Task Force understands IOE has been de-scoped as funding has been cut. SET is currently doing "business process analysis" and does not appear to be moving toward autonomy.

Two promising space system application areas for autonomy are the increased use of autonomy to enable an independent acting system and automation as an augmentation of human operation. In such cases, autonomy's fundamental benefits are to increase a system's operational capability and provide cost savings via increased human labor efficiencies, reducing staffing requirements and increasing mission assurance or robustness to uncertain environments. The automation of human operations, that is, transformation from control with automatic response to autonomy for satellite operations, remains a major challenge. Increased use of autonomy—not only in the number of systems and processes to which autonomous control and reasoning can be applied, but especially in the degree of autonomy that is reflected in these systems and processes—can provide the Air Force with potentially enormous increases in its capabilities. If implemented correctly, this increase has the potential to enable manpower efficiencies and cost reductions.

A potential, yet largely unexplored benefit from adding/increasing autonomous functions could be to increase the ability of space systems to do on-board maintenance via auto-detect, auto-diagnose and auto-tune. Increasing presence of such functionality in space and launch systems can be imagined to reduce the cost of mission assurance by making the systems more adaptive to operational and environmental variations and anomalies.

2.5. Conclusion

Unmanned vehicle technologies, even with limited autonomous capabilities, have proven their value to DoD operations. The development and fielding of air and ground systems, in particular, have helped save lives and extend human capabilities. These systems have especially benefited from a combination of operational demands coupled with general support of senior DoD leadership, who have aided in offsetting the usual bureaucratic process delays in order to accelerate the creation and fielding of these tools for the benefit of today's warfighter.

While positive steps have been made toward advancing UxV capabilities, many areas for improvement remain. Due to the understandable pressures of war, unmanned systems were often fielded before CONOPS were fully developed or understood; deployment support structures (sustainment, service structures, etc.) were immature; and the lack of understanding or validating (testing) maturity to support tactical and operational challenges in remote theaters have further complicated progress.

Among the key challenges going forward (in addition to advancing test and evaluation capabilities to improve trust) for increasing autonomy in unmanned systems is improving data processing capabilities. Identifying more efficient ways of processing the increasing volume of data collected by various platforms will be essential to realizing the platforms' benefits (for example, reduced human costs). In the past, data was collected and distributed to an intelligence analyst community for processing prior to being disseminated to operators in the field. Today, field operators are demanding real-time information, while the intelligence apparatus maintains broader requirements. These competing requirements, along with increasing demands for more information, are straining the current analysis infrastructure. A particular challenge to overcome is the simultaneous distribution of data to meet both specific requests and broader area requirements.

The design approach of current U.S. military autonomous systems is insufficient in light of growing demands for timely, processed information. Current unmanned systems are designed to perform manned operational functions off-board over a communication link, which often results in cumbersome operator control systems, brittle operations and less robust capability than could otherwise be achieved with onboard processing.

The tasks of collecting data with UxVs and processing the data are linked at the systems level through trade-offs of on-board versus off-board sensor data processing. Among the considerations associated with these trade-offs are a manifold of stakeholders with separate and unique requirements. The autonomous system reference framework presented in Chapter 3 will provide a structured way to address these tradeoffs.

The Task Force observes that autonomy has a role in advancing both collection and processing capabilities toward more efficient, integrated ends, such as: operating platforms (from two to many) in concert to improve look angles at priority targets, merging sensor data from multiple vehicles and alternative sources and using both mixed (human/computer) teams and heterogeneous, autonomous agents. However, the current DoD procurement approach of separately acquiring platforms/sensors and sensor processing after downlink is antithetical to achieving an efficient, integrated collection and processing regime. Greater integration for system procurement is required.

The Task Force also notes that key external vulnerability drivers for unmanned systems include communication links, cyber threats and lack of self defense. Internally generated limitations are dominated by software errors, brittleness of physical systems and concerns with collateral damage.

Overall, while the benefits of autonomous systems have made a big impact by complementing human performance in air and ground applications across the DoD, significant room for improvement remains. Both on-board processing and human-assisted algorithms can aid in alleviating data analysis burdens, and significant development and procurement bottlenecks require resolution to accommodate full exploitation of the technology. As operational requirements increasingly rely on autonomous systems, the remediation of these and other exigent issues is imperative.

3.0 Technical Issues of Autonomy

Autonomy is often misunderstood as providing independent thought and action; in fact, for unmanned vehicles it connotes "self-governing." In engineering, the term autonomy originally applied to a mechanical fly-ball controller used to regulate steam engines. In artificial intelligence, the term autonomy implies bounded independent thought and action. As a fundamental principle, Simon's Law of Bounded Rationality[11] states that the actions of a program or robot are bounded by the information it has, the amount of time available for computation and the limitations of its algorithms—thus, the independence of a UxV is fixed by the designers.

Autonomy is **better understood as a capability (or a set of capabilities) that enables the larger human-machine system to accomplish a given mission**, rather than as a "black box" that can be discussed separately from the vehicle and the mission. Examples of common capabilities that computer systems can perform autonomously include generating optimal plans, monitoring plan execution and problem solving, selecting or allocating resources, analyzing data or imagery, implementing or activating the next step in the plan, reacting to the environment to perform the best action and learning. Note that some of the listed capabilities, such as optimal planning, produce better than human results but are not as perceived as taking initiative. Other capabilities—such as a health management system—may take the (bounded) initiative of rerouting signals or applying different control regimes but may not be optimal. Neither optimality nor initiative is sufficient to say one capability is autonomous and the other is intelligent or a "smart" app. For the purposes of this report, a capability that is delegated to the machine is considered autonomous.

Autonomy is also often misunderstood as occurring at the vehicle scale of granularity, rather than at different scales and degrees of sophistication depending on the requirements. This misunderstanding leads to viewing vehicle autonomy as fundamentally distinct from autonomy for "hidden" vehicle capabilities such as resource management or for mission capabilities such as data analysis. Treating vehicle autonomy separately from mission autonomy is at odds with successes in artificial intelligence, which uses the same programming styles, software organization, and test and evaluation methods independently of whether the final result is executed by hardware or software. Separating vehicle and software autonomy impedes cost-effective acquisition of beneficial capabilities, leading to a reinventing-the-wheel syndrome as well as increasing software incompatibility.

Autonomy is, by itself, not a solution to any problem. The utility of an autonomous capability is a function of the ecology of the specific mission needs, the operating environment, the users and the vehicle—there is no value without context. The expectation that autonomy can be added to fix unmanned vehicle design deficits without considering the larger system is flawed.

---

[11] Simon, Herbert A. 1996. The Sciences of the Artificial. 3rd edition. Cambridge, MA: MIT Press.

It is a version of the "a little more technology will be enough, this time" expectation that has been shown to result in negative consequences—such as unanticipated increases in manpower—to deal with the added complexity.[12]

Autonomous capabilities in unmanned systems can reduce the costs of reaching into distant environments and using that reach to meet mission objectives. The Task Force found that research and acquisitions have focused primarily on navigational capabilities, essentially gaining reach, but research and acquisition efforts have not led to developments in perceptual processing, planning, learning, human-robot interaction or multi-agent coordination that would assist in the effective use of that reach.

This chapter begins by identifying what makes autonomy "hard" through the identification of the high-impact technical challenges associated with its implementation. Next, it explains why the levels of autonomy often used to guide development are not useful and offers an autonomous systems reference framework consisting of three classes of design decisions that must be considered: cognitive echelons, mission timelines and human-machine trade spaces. Third, the chapter presents the needed technology development in perceptual processing, planning, learning, human-robot interaction, natural language understanding and multi-agent coordination; it provides an overview of each technology and its benefits, the technology's current state of the art, and gaps. The chapter concludes with a short vision of the future of UxV development, followed by technical recommendations.

3.1. Motivation: What Makes Autonomy Hard

Autonomy is challenging to understand, exploit and develop in part because of the usual issues with innovation, but in part because of its impact on members of the defense enterprise. It is also primarily a software endeavor, which is a shift from traditional hardware oriented, vehicle-centric development.

Autonomy for unmanned systems is a true innovation that is still in its infancy, and advances in unexpected directions are possible. Following the patterns of innovation,[13] it is unlikely that the Department has found the "killer apps" for autonomy. As will be discussed in Chapter 5, adversaries are adopting unmanned systems. Thus, the Department will have to continue to innovate and explore applications as the future systems will not resemble the current unmanned vehicles.

It may be helpful to visualize the challenges of autonomy through the eyes of three key stakeholders: the **commander**, the **operator** and the **developer**. These stakeholders will be referred to throughout the remainder of this chapter.

---

[12] Winograd, T. and D.D. Woods. 1997. Challenges for Human-Centered Design. In Human-Centered Systems: Information, Interactivity, and Intelligence, edited by J. Flanagan, et al. Washington, DC: National Science Foundation.

[13] Rogers, E.M., 2003. Diffusion of Innovations. 5th edition. Free Press.

- For the **commander**, the design space and tradeoffs for incorporating autonomy into a mission are not well understood. Any changes in how missions are accomplished will result in new operational consequences, which the commander must manage.
- For the **operator**, autonomy is experienced as human-machine collaboration, which often is overlooked during design.
- For the **developer**, autonomy is primarily software. Software development is generally outside of the current hardware-oriented, vehicle-centric development and acquisition processes. Program managers may not know how to specify autonomy software, developers may not have sufficient expertise to write autonomy software, and testing and evaluation has few metrics and test beds for verification and validation.

3.2. Defining Levels of Autonomy is Not Useful

The pervasive effort to define autonomy and to create vehicle autonomy roadmaps is counter-productive. The Task Force witnessed the Military Services, and even groups within a Service, making significant investments of time and money to develop definitions of autonomy. The milestones and roadmaps based on computer functions needed for some level of autonomy—rather than to achieve a capability through the best combination of human and machine abilities—foster brittle designs resulting in additional manpower, vulnerabilities and lack of adaptability for new missions. Casting the goal as creating sophisticated functions—rather than creating a joint human-machine cognitive system—reinforces fears of unbounded autonomy and does not prepare commanders to factor into their understanding of unmanned vehicle use that there exist no fully autonomous systems, just as there are no fully autonomous soldiers, sailors, airmen or Marines.

The competing definitions for autonomy have led to confusion among developers and acquisition officers, as well as among operators and commanders. The attempt to define autonomy has resulted in a waste of both time and money spent debating and reconciling different terms and may be contributing to fears of unbounded autonomy. The definitions have been unsatisfactory because they typically try to express autonomy as a *widget* or discrete component, rather than a *capability* of the larger system enabled by the integration of human and machine abilities.

An equally unproductive course has been the numerous attempts to transform conceptualizations of autonomy made in the 1970s into developmental roadmaps. The majority of these efforts appear to rely on popularizations of Sheridan's early work for the National Aeronautics and Space Administration (NASA), which created a taxonomy of human-machine collaboration in order to provide a vocabulary for expressing the state of interaction at any given time during a mission.[14] Sheridan's taxonomy is organized into levels, and is often incorrectly interpreted as implying that autonomy is simply a delegation of a complete task to a

---

[14] Sheridan, Thomas B. 1992. Telerobotics, Automation, and Human Supervisory Control. Cambridge, MA: MIT Press.

computer, that a vehicle operates at a single level of autonomy and that these levels are discrete and represent scaffolds of increasing difficulty.

Though attractive, the conceptualization of levels of autonomy as a scientific grounding for a developmental roadmap has been unproductive for two reasons. First, as noted above, the conceptualization is based on an incorrect understanding of the levels' intent. The levels served as a tool to capture what was occurring in a system to make it autonomous; these linguistic descriptions are not suitable to describe specific milestones of an autonomous system. Second, the road-mapping exercises have not incorporated the corpus of research in autonomy. Research shows that a mission consists of dynamically changing functions, many of which can be executing concurrently as well as sequentially. Each of these functions can have a different allocation scheme to the human or computer at a given time. This dynamic view of human-machine interaction leads back to the definition of autonomy as a capability in which the milestones create the set of interactions needed to produce the desired result.

A negative consequence of the commitment to levels of autonomy is that it deflects focus from the fact that *all autonomous systems are joint human-machine cognitive systems,* thus resulting in brittle designs. Treating the levels of autonomy as a developmental roadmap misses the need to match capabilities with the dynamic needs of the task or mission and directs programming attention away from critical, but implicit, functions needed for overall system resilience and human trust in the system. The mismatch of capabilities leads to gaps in functionality that have to be filled with additional manpower, creates vulnerabilities when unforeseen conditions arise and prevents rapid adaption or re-tasking of unmanned systems for new missions. Programming attention to the machine often means a lack of focus on the interfaces and tools that confirm to the operators and commanders that the system is performing mission priorities; without these interfaces and tools, there is no trust in the overall system.

Another negative consequence of framing autonomy as levels is that it reinforces fears about unbounded autonomy. Treating autonomy as a widget or "black box" supports an "us versus the computer" attitude among commanders rather than the more appropriate understanding that *there are no fully autonomous systems just as there are no fully autonomous soldiers, sailors, airmen or Marines.* Perhaps the most important message for commanders is that all systems are supervised by humans to some degree, and the best capabilities result from the coordination and collaboration of humans and machines.

3.3. Autonomous System Reference Framework

A candidate reference framework was developed by the Task Force and is presented in Figure 3-1. It is intended to illustrate the concept and to provide the Department with a point of departure for efforts to refine and adopt this structure across all DoD autonomous systems programs. The framework captures the three classes of design decisions for autonomy that meet the above criteria and provides the visibility to ensure that they are addressed explicitly during the requirements specification, design and review/approval phases of the acquisition process. A design should be examined from each of these three classes: the **cognitive echelon view**, the **mission timelines view** in which autonomy may assist in different ways at key moments such as takeoff and landing, and the **human-machine system trades space view** in which factors influencing performance, reliability, manpower, training costs and adoption are explicitly considered.

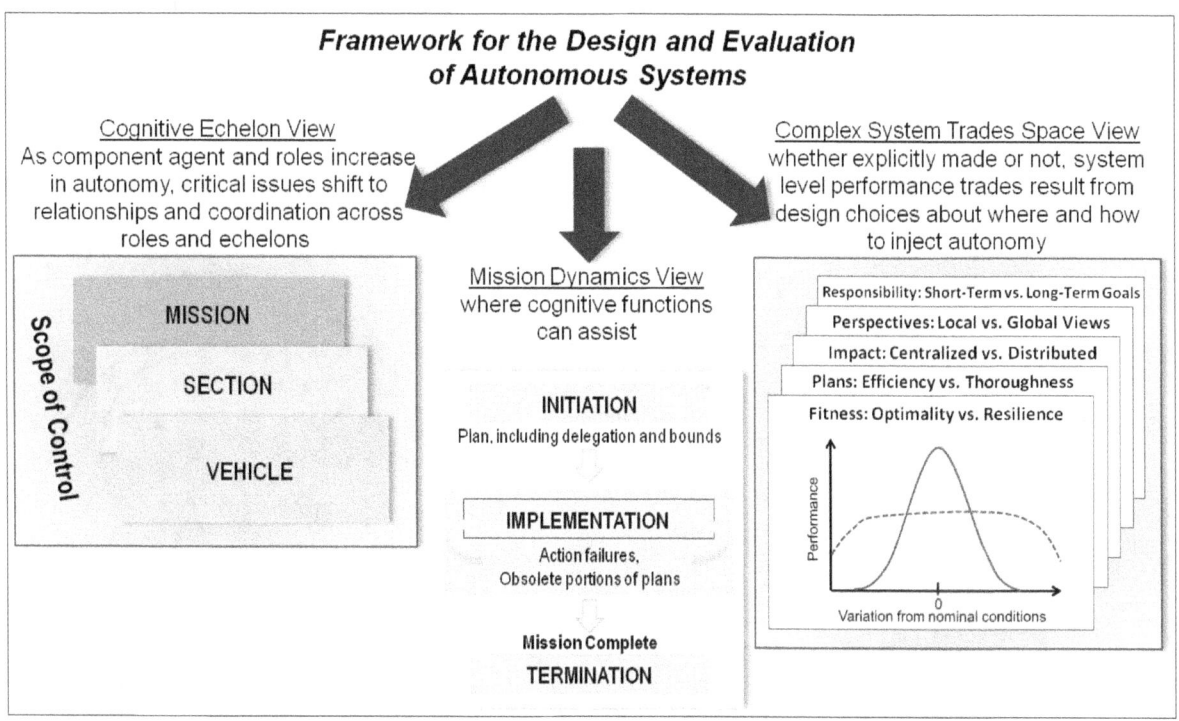

Figure 3-1 Framework for the Design and Evaluation of Autonomous Systems

3.3.1. Cognitive Echelon View

The potential benefits and challenges of autonomy will vary with the types of decisions being made. The cognitive echelon view provides a framework to more explicitly capture these potential benefits from the perspective of users with different spans of control, from vehicle pilot to mission level commander. It also helps elicit opportunities for the additional use of autonomy. Many systems today focus on the incorporation of autonomy at the vehicle level where the interaction is with pilots and sensor operators. Autonomy is used to translate higher-level route waypoints into vehicle trajectories and control actions, to point and track sensors against targets and to process raw sensor data into higher levels of information content, such as target tracks.

Autonomy can also be employed at vehicle mission levels in which planning tools can support team leaders and their staff in generating potential courses of action and mission management functions to monitor execution, identify actual or incipient failures and facilitate coordination of operations among companion vehicles and teammates.

At even higher levels, the focus shifts toward management of resources against high-level mission objectives. Today, large-scale resource and task allocation, such as tasking dozens of platforms—each with multiple options for sensors and weapon load outs and platform assignments—against dozens of targets, are often undertaken in a largely manual fashion. The scale of these large allocation and tasking functions present significant time and manpower challenges for mission commanders and their staff. Such large-scale operations are well suited for optimization-based planning tools, offering the promise of reducing pre-mission timelines, manpower and workload while delivering better use of mission. Situational awareness functions at this echelon level are less about vehicles and more about capturing an understanding of the complex, and at times, rapidly, evolving battlespace. Intelligent analysis software can help mission commanders in sorting through the ever growing volume of data to extract relevant and actionable information.

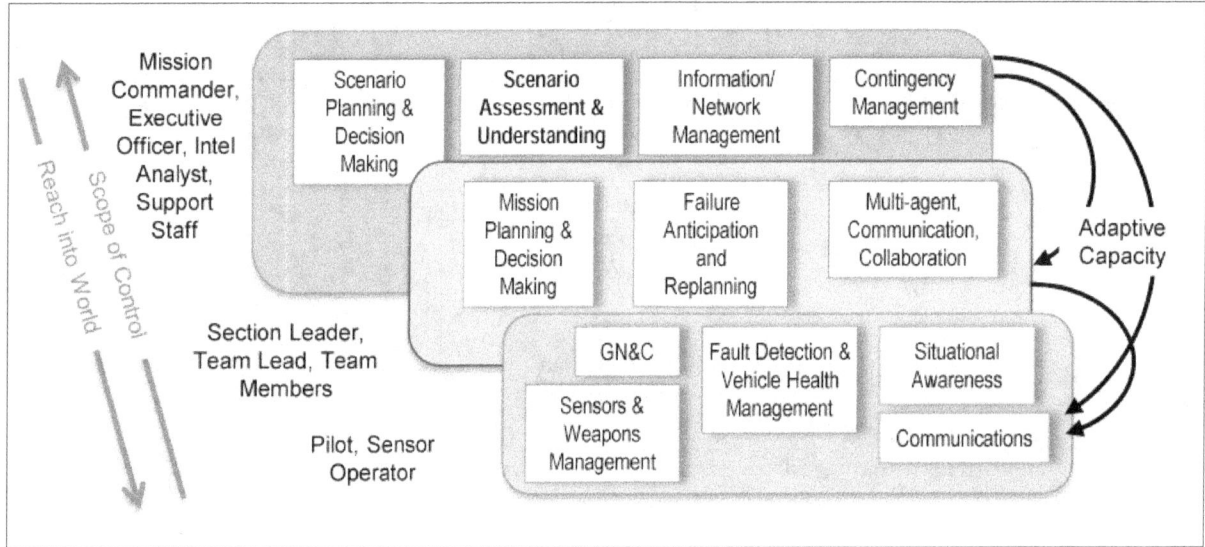

Figure 3-2 Autonomous System Reference Framework–Scope of Cognitive Functionality Across Echelons

This framework helps to capture more explicitly not only where autonomy is being used, but also where manual implementation is currently employed. This helps identify promising paths for insertion of additional autonomy that can improve overall system performance and enhance mission capability while at the same time reducing manpower and workload.

3.3.2. Timeline View

While the potential benefits and challenges of autonomy will vary with the types of decisions being made, it is important to remember that decision types change over the timeline of a mission. As illustrated in Figure 3-3, a typical mission may have an initiation phase followed by an implementation and termination phase. Each phase represents a different opportunity for autonomy. For example, the initiation phase may exploit autonomous planning algorithms for pre-flight functions, including path planning and contingency plans, and it may also support more sophisticated mission planning such as specifying permissible delegation of authority and bounds on actions. Another example of autonomy in the initiation phase is autonomous takeoff. The implementation phase of unmanned system missions is the nominal, or steady-state, case for the mission. Unmanned aerial vehicles often rely on autonomous waypoint navigation. However, autonomy can provide further benefits by leveraging software agents to monitor for action failures or changing situations which may render portions of an initial plan obsolete and require replanning. In the termination phase, once a mission is complete, autonomy can be used to preprocess collected data, return the vehicle home, and autonomously land.

The key point is that humans and computer agents will interchange initiative and roles across mission phases and echelons to adapt to new events, disruptions and opportunities as situations evolve. Autonomy can assist with the continuous cycle of sensing, acting and planning.

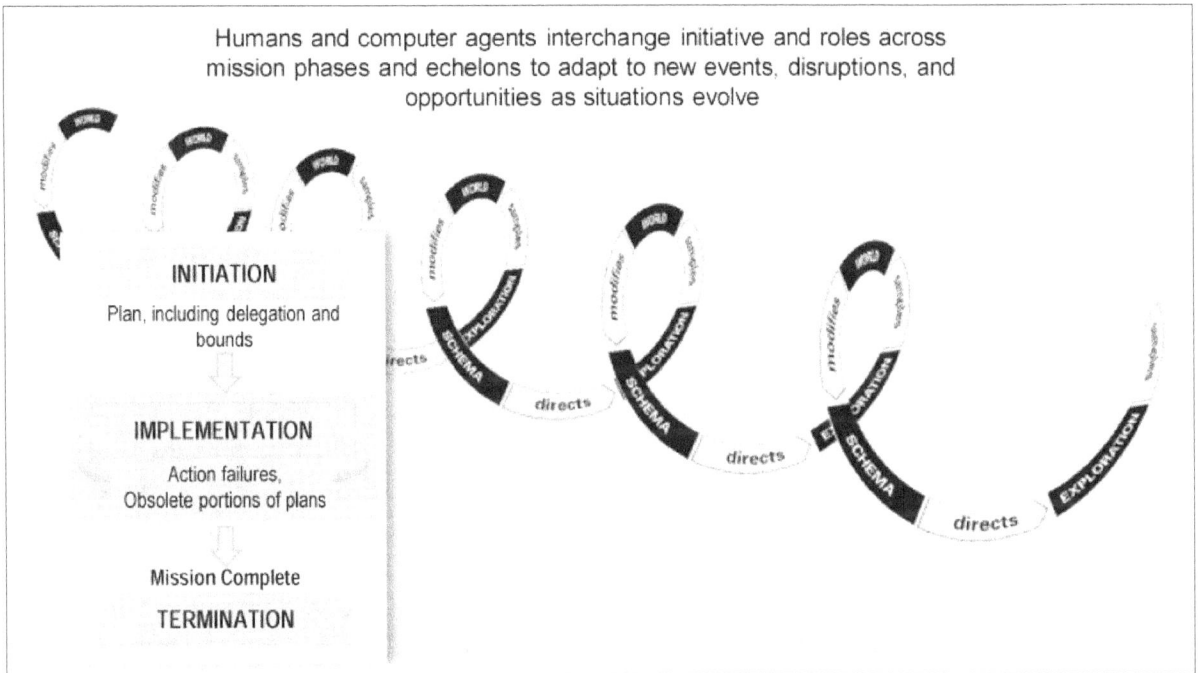

Figure 3-3 Autonomous System Reference Framework – Timeline View

3.3.3. Human-Machine System Trade Space View

The trade space view is helpful tool for predicting unintended consequences and linking symptoms of imbalances (higher manpower, breakdowns, increase in human error, etc.) with the source. The trade space view models autonomy with a balloon metaphor: autonomy can increase the capability or capacity of a system, but that there are also five tradeoffs that can "pop the balloon" or limit its expansion if not explicitly addressed. These five trade spaces are:

- **Fitness**, or how well the system balances the need for optimal performance for expected missions with the need for resilience and adaptability for new missions or unexpected conditions.
- **Plans**, or how efficient the system is in following an existing plan balanced with the need to detect when a plan is no longer valid and adapt.

- **Impact**, or how the information from both the distant and local perspectives is made visible without becoming vulnerable to hidden or obscured aspects.
- **Perspectives**, or the ability to understand the situation, balancing concentrating action in one unit with distributing and coordinating across multiple units for greater effect.
- **Responsibility**, or balancing short term with long term goals and resolving goal conflicts.

The five trade spaces are summarized in Table 3-1 below. Each trade space captures how increases in capability from additional autonomy can inadvertently introduce unintended consequences and missed opportunities in overall system performance. The discussion provides examples of situations in which the Task Force saw an autonomous capability injected into unmanned vehicles that produced unintended consequences. Autonomy will be more successfully introduced with less risk if the consequences across the multiple trade spaces are considered early, thus allowing for identification of early warning signs of unintended consequences and ways to counter-balance or re-balance system performance across the trade spaces.

The **fitness** trade space captures trade-offs between optimality and resilience. Adding autonomous capabilities may lead to optimal algorithms, which provide more precision and effective results. However, algorithms are only optimal for well-understood or completely modeled situations. One unintended consequence may be an increase in brittleness, which could hamper a system's ability to adapt to inevitable surprises. An imbalance between optimality and resilience also leads to missed opportunities, particularly the ability to adapt and keep pace with the changing world. The new capability encourages decision makers to operate near the edge of new capacity boundaries to reach new goals, which undermines resilience. Three warning signs of an imbalance in this trade space are: occasional surprising breakdowns, higher manpower or higher training costs than promised and creeping complexity costs. One example of this is how UAV CONOPS changed from reconnaissance, surveillance, and target acquisition (RSTA) functions, with an expectation of 20 orbits, to a demand for integrated sensor coverage area (ISCA) with 85 orbits, 24-hours a day, seven days a week. These demands have exceeded the designed capacity and, as a result, it is not uncommon to have 170 people supporting a combat air patrol. Creating a balanced fitness for the ecology requires a formal measure of brittleness, design guidelines to produce human-machine systems with greater capacities for resilience and mechanisms for coordinating across multiple echelons and units of action when surprises occur.

Table 3-1 Autonomous System Reference Framework--Complex System Trades Space View

Trade Space	Trades	Benefits	Unintended Consequences
Fitness	Optimality vs. resilience	More precise for understood situations	Increased brittleness
Plans	Efficiency vs. thoroughness	Balanced use of computational resources	Locked into wrong plan/difficulty revising plan
Impact	Centralized vs. distributed	Ability to tailor actions to appropriate echelon	High cost of coordination
Perspectives	Local vs. global views	Ability to balance scale/area of action with resolution	Data overload; reduced speed of decision making
Responsibility	Short-term vs. long-term goals	Builds trust by tailoring risk management to goals, priorities, context	Break down in collaboration and coordination

The **plans** trade space reflects the interplay between efficiency and thoroughness. Efficiency is often focused on the expected, sacrificing a thorough examination of the situation. The benefit of efficiency is that it minimizes computational resources by exploiting knowledge and expectations. However, this can lead to the system pursuing a plan that is no longer valid because the assumptions enabling efficient operations prevent the system from detecting that the situation has changed. Even if the system (or operator) notices the plan is no longer valid, the efficient algorithm may not be thorough enough to find a useful revision to the plan. Warning signs of an imbalance include missing leading indicators of trouble or bottlenecks, following a plan not matched to the current situation and recognizing the plan doesn't fit the situation at hand but falls back on ad hoc replanning that misses important constraints. Balancing this trade space requires the capability to understand intent, to use intent to autonomously monitor and adapt plans to situations and to autonomously enlist more computational resources or employ different algorithms when situations challenge plans and progress.

The **impact** trade space expresses the balance between centralization and distribution of decision-making and information resources; it essentially focuses efforts on determining when to concentrate action in one unit versus distributing and coordinating across multiple units for greater effect. For example, in stealth missions, the UxV may have more onboard autonomy. Imbalances between centralized and distributed control often result in a high cost of increased manpower to manage the coordination. Warning signs of imbalance in this tradespace are high cost of coordination, which leads to underutilization, unjustified mistrust in distributed control, which also leads to underutilization, over-trust in delegation to UxVs, which leads to surprises, operators missing side effects of actions because they cannot maintain comprehension of the distributed assets and too much centralization, which leads to platform micromanagement. Balancing this tradespace requires advances in representing and expressing UxV activities, increased problem solving, planning and scheduling capabilities to enable dynamic tasking of distributed UxVs and tools for fluent synchronization of human and UxV roles.

The **perspectives** trade space, or how easy it is to understand the situation, reflects a balance between local and global views of the battlespace. Autonomous systems can extend and prolong reach and perceive distant environments, allowing the warfighter to obtain information at a desired scale or over an area of interest. However, perception at one scale obscures or distracts from perception at another. An imbalance in local and global views can take what should be automatic perceptual comprehension of the situation and forces the warfighter to make slow, and often error-prone, deliberative inferences about the environment. Imbalances also make it difficult to find the interesting events and changes. Yet another unintended consequence is data overload, which reduces the speed of decision-making. For example, the increase in data collected by the Predator led to a 30% increase in the number of analysts needed to sort through its data, yet only 5% of the data collected by the Predator makes it to the dismounted soldier. Increased autonomy in perception and reasoning can help match the highly accurate local data with the larger global understanding. Balancing the perspicuity trade space requires perceptual and attentional interfaces that intelligently assist the human to manage and navigate through multiple perspectives and sensor feeds and computer vision and autonomous reasoning to continuously identify and refocus attention on high relevance events.

The **responsibility** trade space captures disparity between short-term and long-term goals. The correct delegation of responsibilities to the UxV for short term and long term goals is that it builds trust in the system, allows the warfighter to focus on overarching mission goals and keeps the priorities on the mission—and not on managing the UxV. This delegation is critical; as UxVs become more capable and are used in more demanding situations, they will be delegated more tasks. Unintended consequences of poorly distributed responsibility include increased costs: consider that 30% of the costs of operating the Predator could be reduced if the responsibility for takeoff and landing were shifted from the human to the unmanned system. Warning signs of an imbalance in this trade space include avoidable collateral damage in friendly fire events, failure of systems that are attributed to human error, mistrust or over-trust in the UxV by groups responsible for monitoring the safe envelope of operations and groups shifting risk (or blame) associated with the UxV across units and echelons. Balancing the delegation of responsibility requires autonomous capabilities to be designed according to new laws of responsible robotics[15] and advances in expressing the bounds on an autonomous capability and its ability to respond adaptively.

---

[15] Murphy, R. R. and D.D. Woods. 2009. Beyond Asimov: The Three Laws of Responsible Robotics. IEEE Intelligent Systems 24(4): 14-20.

3.4. Needed Technology Development

Autonomy presents opportunities to expand mission capability with a mix of existing technologies and needed developments. This section revisits the cognitive echelon view to provide examples of underutilized existing capability and open technical challenges needing investment.

In order to maintain consistency with the source material and to avoid adding to the large set of ad hoc definitions already mudding understanding of autonomy, this section of the report uses the somewhat confusing scientific terminology to describe the state of art and the gaps in each of the key technology enablers. The terminology stems from the history of robotics, in which robot development for factory automation focused on control theory for precise, repetitive movements of factory arms in well-modeled environments (i.e., motor skills in the cerebellum of the central nervous system) while mobile robots developed for planetary exploration focused on artificial intelligence (i.e., the cerebrum).[16] Note that the styles are complementary, just as the cerebellum and cerebrum work together. The emerging principles in artificial intelligence for mobile robots were adopted for use by software-only autonomy, especially web-based applications. As a result, artificial intelligence refers to the common core of programming principles as "agency." If it is necessary to identify that an algorithm is restricted to a particular type of agent, AI refers to a mobile robot as a "physically-situated agent" to distinguish it from a "software agent," and "robot" is reserved for a system using the factory automation style of programming. With the increasing adoption of what had been previously called mobile robots, DoD has adopted the term "unmanned system." Given the pervasiveness of the term "unmanned system" in DoD programs, this section will use "unmanned system," UxV, etc., wherever possible unless its use would interfere with locating a concept in the scientific literature for further reading.

The Task Force identified six key areas in which advances in autonomy would have significant benefit to the unmanned system: perception, planning, learning, human-robot interaction, natural language understanding and multi-agent coordination. These enabling areas are described briefly in terms of their benefits, followed by the state of the art and gaps that require research investment. To summarize the status across these key technical areas, Figure 3-4 uses the cognitive echelon view of the reference framework to highlight areas where existing capability is underutilized and where additional research is needed. Before discussing the areas in detail, the underutilization of existing capability is illustrated by providing a concrete example of how they arise in the UAV setting.

Small, soldier-operated UAVs are an example of systems that underutilize autonomy. Such fielded systems operate either through direct teleoperation or with a handful of Global Positioning System GPS waypoints. Users are interested in information from the UAV sensors for a given mission objective. These systems are often operated by two people, one flies the

---

[16] Murphy, R.R. 2000. Introduction to AI Robotics. Cambridge, MA: MIT Press.

UAV and the other monitors the raw video returns. Existing autonomy technology can be used for such systems to:

- Replace a two full-time person team with a single, part-time operator who is assigned multiple units.
- Task a system at the mission level. For example, a soldier can task the system to find a specified class of objects for a defined region. The mission capability autonomy software can then factor in the UAV's flight performance characteristics, sensor field of view, resolution properties and terrain conditions to generate desired flight trajectories.
- Alert the operator to modeled objects of interest through autonomous data processing. This would avoid the need to manually observe raw video returns, a task which can potentially result in hours of operation.

The net result is a significantly reduced workload and improvements in human-system performance. This level of automation is sometimes available for larger UAV systems, but the processing requirements for such autonomy software is well within the capabilities of today's laptops and embedded processors and is therefore ready for insertion into these smaller systems.

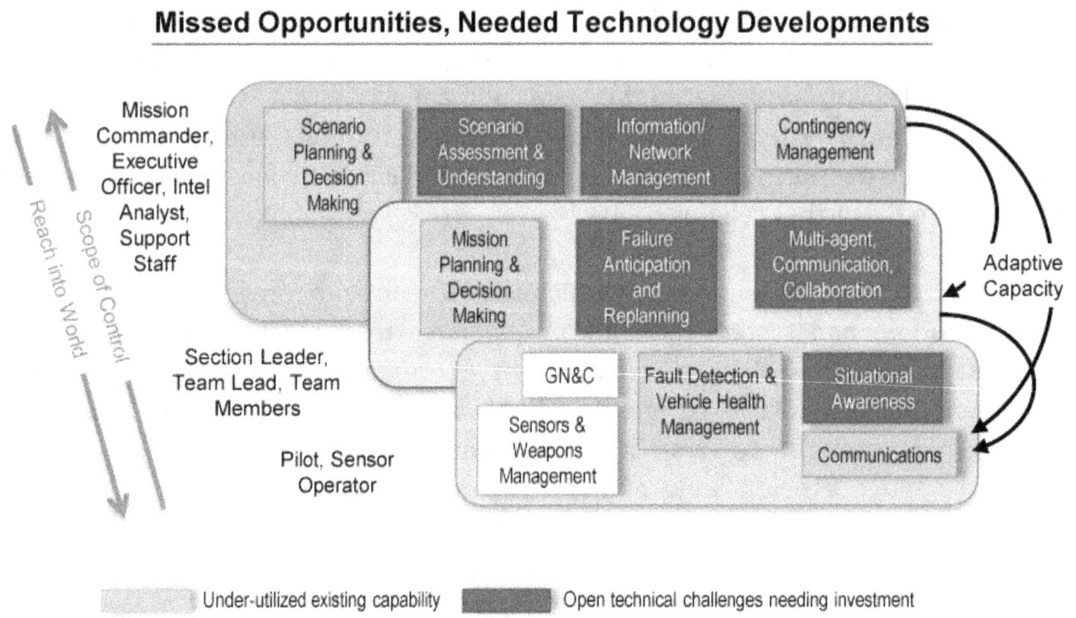

Figure 3-4 Status of Technology Deployment and Remaining Challenges

3.4.1. Perception

Perception is essential for autonomy, for enabling the unmanned vehicle to achieve reach (e.g., navigate through environments and manipulate obstacles) and for using reach to meet mission objectives, either for a platform (e.g., collecting sensor data, applying kinetic weapons, defeating IEDs) or for the battlespace.

Perception consists of sensors (hardware) and sensing (software). A sensor modality refers to what the raw input to the sensor is:[17] sound, pressure, temperature, light and so on. In some regards, modalities are similar to the five senses in humans. A modality can be further subdivided. For instance, vision can be decomposed into visible light, infrared light, X-rays and other modalities. Processing for navigation and mission sensors is called computer vision if the sensor modality uses the electromagnetic spectrum to produce an image. An image represents data in a picture-like format with a direct physical correspondence to the scene being captured. For the purposes of this discussion, perception for unmanned systems will be divided into four categories based on purpose: navigation, mission sensing, system health and manipulation. The categories are not completely distinct as a platform may need to manipulate a door in order to navigate indoors or it may need to manipulate an IED to complete its mission. Further, navigation is associated with achieving reach and moving in a denied area, while mission sensing is for using the reach afforded by navigation to accomplish objectives.

Referencing the components in Figure 1-1, perception for navigation is needed for guidance, navigation and control (GN&C) functions, to support path planning and dynamic replanning and to enable multi-agent communication and coordination. Navigation generally refers to the overall progress of the platform towards a goal, as opposed to the control of the mobility of the platform (such as staying upright or the selection of gaits in legged robots). One advantage of increasing navigational perception is vehicle safety—humans often cannot react fast enough or overcome the network lags to maintain reliable or safe navigation. A second advantage is that navigational perception can reduce the cognitive workload of operating or piloting the vehicle, though this alone may not be sufficient to reduce manpower needs. If the perception processing resides onboard, the platform can react faster as well as be resistant to network denial attacks or degradations.

Perception for mission sensing is needed for mission planning, scenario planning, assessment and understanding, multi-agent communication and coordination and situational awareness. Increasing autonomous perception for mission sensing offers four significant benefits for the enterprise. First, it can enable the robot to covertly conduct a mission, such as tracking an activity, without constant network connectivity. This reduces network vulnerabilities and cognitive workload on operators. Second, autonomous recognition, or even cueing and prioritization of areas of interest, can reduce the large number of analysts needed to deal with the data avalanche. Third, onboard identification, or even partial prioritization of data to be sent, can reduce the network demands, as exemplified by Global Hawk's large consumption of bandwidth. And fourth, mission perception can be linked to navigation, for example, directing the platform to hover, stare, circle, etc.

---

[17] Geyer, C.M., S. Singh, and L.J. Chamberlain. 2008. Avoiding Collisions Between Aircraft: State of the Art and Requirements for UAVs operating in Civilian Airspace. tech. report CMU-RI-TR-08-03.

Perception of the vehicle's health is needed primarily for fault detection and vehicle health management, but it is also required for failure anticipation and replanning and contingency management. Increased autonomous health monitoring has at least three advantages. First, it can support graceful degradation of performance and recovery from faults as autonomous fault detection, identification and recovery is likely to be faster than a human. Second, it increases trust in the system, specifically that the system will not behave unexpectedly or fail suddenly during a critical phase of the mission. Third, it may further reduce cognitive workload of operators, freeing them from watching the diagnostic displays.

Perception for manipulation has become more important as navigation has moved from outdoors to indoors and missions have moved from perceiving at a distance to acting at a distance. Opening a door with a ground robot is a major challenge. Other missions now include IED disposal, car inspection, which involves moving blankets or packages, and logistics and materials handling. Increased autonomous perception for manipulation offers two advantages. First, it decreases the time and workload needed for manipulation tasks. Second, it can reduce the number of robots needed for a mission, as often a second robot is used to help the operator better see the relationship of the manipulator to the object being manipulated.

3.4.1.1.   State of the Art

The state of the art in perception highlights missed opportunities, three of which would have significant impact on enabling UxV missions. One is for UAVs to use onboard computer vision algorithms to a) reduce the data avalanche that overwhelms network bandwidth and analysts and b) sense and avoid. The second is for UGVs to exploit existing mechanisms for sensing wireless network quality and move to maintain or extend the network. The third is for UAVs and UGVs to use human computation, or computer-assisted human recognition and understanding, rather than the current "all or nothing" approach to reconnaissance and surveillance.

The state of the art in perception for the navigational, mission, system health and manipulation categories reflects a spectrum, where navigation is the most mature and mobile manipulation is emerging as a distinct area of investigation. The state of the art in navigational sensing can be summarized as: active range sensors are used for ground obstacle avoidance and mapping, while obstacle avoidance sensing for aerial and underwater vehicles remains a challenge. UGVs currently rely heavily on range sensors, such as LADAR, LIDAR, stereo-vision and the RGB-R sensors (Microsoft Kinect) for navigation. These sensors may be susceptible to environmental effects such as changes in lighting and the presence of dust, smoke or fog. The most popular and reliable range sensors use lasers, which introduce the possibility of detection by adversaries. The state of the art in UAV navigational sensing has demonstrated the sense-and-avoid capabilities using passive computer vision as well as active sensing.[18] The Office of Naval Research biologically-inspired flow field computation for sensing and control of ground vehicles

---

[18] Geyer, C.M., S. Singh, and L.J. Chamberlain. 2008. Avoiding Collisions Between Aircraft: State of the Art and Requirements for UAVs operating in Civilian Airspace. tech. report CMU-RI-TR-08-03.

on optical flow is expected to leverage advances in computational power, neurophysiological and cognitive studies to duplicate robust depth perception found in animals. The state of the art in UMV navigational sensing appears to remain based on sonar, Doppler velocity logging, and a priori knowledge, with some investigations of optical flow.

The state of the art in mission sensing can be summarized as follows: well-specified objects or events can be autonomously recognized under favorable conditions, while cues and indicators of areas of interest can be generated under less-constrained conditions for rapid disambiguation by human analysts. Significant progress has been made in fusing geolocated imagery from multiple sources, most notably the open source Photosynth, which was developed for public imagery. Perception for temporal (activity) understanding remains limited. Promising work is being done in human interaction with computer vision processing, also referred to as "human computation,"[19] which can reduce manpower and cognitive workload, while reducing false negatives due to humans missing objects or events. These are excellent examples of human-system collaboration being used effectively to achieve mission objectives.

The state of the art in platform health is based on a rich set of literature on model-based fault detection and recovery from general hardware and software failures as well as the detection and recovery of loss of network connectivity. Internal fault detection and identification does not appear to be a major focus for unmanned systems, with the exception of the Defense Advanced Research Projects Agency (DARPA) Damage Tolerant Controls program. That program demonstrated an autonomous subscale F-18 adapting to the loss of a wing.[20] The state of the art for perceptive system health monitoring for navigation and mission functions is exemplified by the NASA Deep Space One probe, which used model-based detection and recovery to detect errors in software execution as well as malfunctions or damage to hardware.[21] A major health impact is loss of wireless network connectivity. The networked robotics and multi-robot systems communities have generally taken three different approaches to loss of communications: proactively preventing sustained networked loss by pre-placing repeaters or deploying as needed, opportunistic dual-use of land, sea and aerial mobile resources (including soldiers), which can serve as repeaters and providing sufficient onboard autonomy so that the vehicle does not have to rely on network connectivity to a centralized controller. The concept of proactively placing repeaters or using mobile resources as repeaters has been examined by numerous DoD programs; a recent example of this is the DARPA LANdroids program.[22] The Space and Naval Warfare Systems Command (SPAWAR) developed a set of automatically deployed communication relays (ADCR) compatible with mounting on an iRobot Packbot. Despite winning the Outstanding Technology Development award from the Federal Laboratory

---

[19] Human Computation Workshop (HCOMP). in AAAI Annual Conference on Artificial Intelligence.

[20] Jourdan, D.B., et al. 2010. Enhancing UAV Survivability Through Damage Tolerant Control in Proceedings of the AIAA Guidance Navigation and Control Conference. AIAA.

[21] Bernard D, Doyle R, Riedel E., Rouquette N, Wyatt J, Lowry M & Nayak P (1999). Autonomy and software technology on NASA's Deep Space One. 1999. Intelligent Systems. May/June: 10-1 5.

[22] McClurea, M., D.R. Corbettb, and D.W. Gage. 2009. The DARPA LANdroids program. in SPIE Unmanned Systems Technology XI. SPIE.

Consortium, Far West Region in 2008, and being commercialized, the system does not appear to have been widely adopted.[23]

The state of the art in mobile manipulation is to have a human in the loop operate a single manipulator arm while the base platform remains stationary or slowly approaches the object of interest. The description of the currently active DARPA Autonomous Robotic Manipulation (ARM) program[24] captures many of the challenges in mobile manipulation, including grasping, multi-arm grasping and grasping and moving at the same time. Mobile manipulation is especially challenging as it is essentially two distinct problems. Based on an animal perception model, mobile manipulation is generally divided into two phases: approach and grasping, each with different perception. The approach phase relies on vision or range sensing to identify and track handles, doorknobs or objects of interest. Grasping is informed by haptic sensing, both touch (tactile) and positioning of the effectors. Haptics was recognized by the Institute of Electrical and Electronics Engineers (IEEE) in 2009 as a distinct research community, suggesting that realizable advances may be imminent.

3.4.1.2. Gaps
The Task Force finds critical gaps in five areas:

Perception and situational awareness to operate in a complex battle space. Perceptual programs appear to concentrate on increasing navigational autonomy for individual or related swarms of platforms. Perception for vehicle missions appears to be a secondary priority.

1. Integrating the perceptions of the individual platforms for understanding the battlespace was not in evidence beyond representing positions with map iconography. Perception to support human comprehension of the platform state and to project its relation to the battlespace and mission objectives is largely ignored and instead erroneously treated as a computer display problem; however, a display cannot compensate for the lack of sensing.
2. *Airspace deconfliction for dense manned-unmanned system operations.* As discussed in section 3.10.1, sense-and-avoid has been examined and many solutions appear to exist. The primary gap appears to be less in the fundamental theory but rather in hardening these solutions and integrating them with existing technologies and within socio-organizational constraints.
3. *Real-time pop-up threat detection and identification.* Threat detection and identification can be viewed as the highest level of situational awareness, in which the warfighter can identify and project needed action. Threats can be either detected by onboard

---

[23] Automatically Deployed Communication Relays (ADCR) Available from:
http://www.public.navy.mil/spawar/Pacific/Robotics/Pages/ADCR.aspx
[24] Autonomous Robotic Manipulation (ARM). 2012 Mar 29, 2012]; Available from:
http://www.darpa.mil/Our_Work/DSO/Programs/Autonomous_Robotic_Manipulation_%28ARM%29.aspx

perceptual systems for an individual platform or by integration with observations from multiple platforms and information from other sources.

4. *High-speed obstacle detection in complex terrain.* UGV navigation in urban environments, in dense foliage off road and with people remains nascent.

5. *Multi-sensor integration.* Perception for unmanned systems generally relies on a single sensor per capability, for example a range sensor for autonomous navigation and a camera for mission payloads. Multi-sensor integration, either for increased sensing certainty or more comprehensive world modeling, appears to be ignored.

In addition to these areas, three other gaps are discussed below: the gap between investments in sensing versus in sensors, the gap in the capabilities of evidential reasoning methods for reliable sensing and vehicle health monitoring and the gap in sensing for manipulation.

Sensing Versus Sensors. The Task Force observed that programs appeared to have one or more of three counterproductive attributes that produced gaps in sensing. The most counterproductive tendency is to focus on the development of new sensors rather than on advancing algorithms for existing sensors, particularly vision. The push for more computer vision research is particularly relevant given that the successful Microsoft Kinect uses a noisy range sensor combined with refinements of computer vision and machine learning algorithms that have been present in the scientific literature for decades. While the investment in hardened sensor processing for the Kinect was significant, the point is that the theory already existed but required a final, but non-trivial, investment to transfer into practice. Another tendency is to view perception as either all-human or all-computer; this ignores human computation solutions where the human and the computer cooperatively perceive. The third is for programs, most notably UAV sense-and-avoid, that require autonomous perception to exceed human performance. Of these three, the focus on new sensors over sensor processing is the most significant.

An example of the gap between sensors and sensor processing is the lack of high-speed obstacle detection in complex terrain. UGV navigation generally relies on sensing range directly rather than from stereo, motion or other biomimetic cues. While these specialized range sensors permit rapid identification of surfaces for navigation, it is not sufficient to permit the UGV to determine the difference between a bush and a rock. Rather, it must distinguish among a bush that it can run over, tall weeds that indicate a drop off into a creek bed underneath and the presence of a rock among the weeds that would damage it. While the DARPA Learning Applied to Ground Robotics (LAGR) program has made progress in the bush versus rock arena for large UGVs, range sensing does not compare to the rich information extracted by the human visual perceptual system.

A benefit of investing in advanced sensing beyond enabling navigational autonomy is enabling useful information to be extracted and distributed in time to allow the desired effects to be accomplished. Time delays accrue from the need to have human analysts interpret data and the volume of data that has to be transmitted over networks for offboard processing. This manpower allocation and accrued latency could be reduced by onboard sensing algorithms that perform recognition of key objects or conditions, filter or prioritize data and adapt the distribution of data to network availability. Specialized graphics processors designed specifically for vision algorithms can overcome the inefficiencies of general purpose computer chips that exacerbate the computational complexity of most vision algorithms. Explicit system integration of human computation is a near-term solution that should be explored.

One topic for advanced sensing processing should be the *symbol-ground problem*, or how to extract information and create symbolic representations with semantic meaning. Advances in the symbol-ground problem are needed for navigational perception; these include spatial reasoning and matching current surroundings to a priori map information and mission perception such as autonomous object recognition, activity detection and imagery labeling.

Evidential Reasoning About Sensing and Vehicle Health. Evidential reasoning is needed to allocate the most effective sensor and algorithm combinations for a context and to fuse sensor data while remaining sensitive to the possibility of sensor failures or spoofed readings such as pop up threat detection. Evidential reasoning has been successful for isolating independent faults in completely modeled, "closed world" systems, but much work remains to be done in detecting, identifying and recovering from multiple dependent faults so that the vehicle can both continue to navigate and maximize mission performance. Another issue is creating an model of the system accurate enough to support evidential reasoning; research is needed on how partial models of the world and the system can still be effectively exploited to provide graceful degradation.

Probabilistic methods that fueled recent advances in simultaneous localization and mapping may not generalize to mission sensing and vehicle health because many methods are susceptible to sensor noise and to "black swan" situations that have low probability but high negative consequences. Probabilistic methods tend to not scale well to complex environments, leading to high demands on memory and computation power. It should be emphasized that outdoor navigation relies on GPS that may not be available or accurate due to urban canyons or area denial operations, illustrating the need for autonomous self-monitoring for anomalous perception.

Manipulation. Perception for manipulation is a major gap for UGV, and to a lesser degree UMV, navigation and mission. The lack of autonomous perception or autonomous perception combined with human computation results in longer times to complete tasks, more errors and increased operator workload. A major problem is that the level of physical dexterity and sensors for perceptual competence for mobile manipulation is currently unknown, though this is being explored by the DARPA Autonomous Robotic Manipulation (ARM) program.

3.4.2. Planning
Planning is the process of computing a sequence or partial order of actions that change the world from the current state to a desired state, or in DoD terminology, a plan is a course of

action designed to achieve mission objectives while minimizing resource utilization. The process relies on two key components: 1) a representation of actions, descriptions of conditions in the world and objectives/resource optimization criteria and 2) algorithms for computing action sequences and assigning resources to the actions so as to conform to the hard constraints of the problem (e.g., vehicle limitations in terms of terrain and speed) while optimizing the soft constraints (e.g., minimizing the total mission time or personnel use).

Planning has been applied in a wide variety of settings: commercial/industrial, governmental and military. Manufacturing has long exploited planning for logistics and matching product demand to production schedules through a range of commercial products. For example, the Engineering Works & Traffic Information Management System (ETMS) was developed to plan and manage maintenance and repair work for the Hong Kong subway system[25]. Bell et al. (2009) developed an AI planning system for devising and monitoring voltage targets in a power system in the U.K. NASA has developed and deployed several systems that employ AI planning. The *Autonomous Sciencecraft Experiment* analyzes experiment results onboard earth observing satellites and replans to address problems or exploit opportunities (Sherwood et al. 2007). The Multi-Rover Integrated Science Understanding System (MISUS) was designed to coordinate data gathering plans across a team of autonomous rovers (Estlin et al. 2005). Monterey Bay Aquarium's Research Institute has been developing the T-REX (Teleo-Reactive-Executive) system to control underwater autonomous systems on data collection missions (McGann et al. 2008). On Time Systems developed the ARGOS system to help plan to build new Navy vessels and developed a system to route all Air Force non-combat flights to reduce fuel consumption (On Time Systems 2012).

AI planning supports the management of complex systems in which optimization is both critical and difficult to achieve; it also provides the algorithms needed to make decisions about action (provide autonomy) in situations in which humans are not in the environment (e.g., space, the ocean).

3.4.2.1. State of the Art

The state of the art described below highlights the missed opportunities to take advantage of increases in efficiency and knowledge engineering that would eliminate the need for extensive manual mission configuration inputs (such as GPS waypoints, communication frequencies, power/fuel constraints, etc.) by the operator and allow planning to be performed by the vehicle or on the operator's control unit rather than at a remote centralized server. The incorporation of planning algorithms would not only provide near optimal plans in real-time, but it would also reduce operator training and workload.

---

[25] Chun, Andy, et al. 2005. Scheduling Engineering Works for the MTR Corporation in Hong Kong; American Association for Artificial Intelligence.

Recent advances in planning have been driven by several factors. First, the community developed a common representation, Planning Domain Definition Language (PDDL)[26]. It was first proposed in 1998 and has been significantly extended since then to expand its expressiveness. In particular, the language has incorporated more sophisticated models of time and objectives (Fox et al. 2003), events beyond the control of the planner,[27] preferences[28]and probabilities.[29] The common representation has expedited faster development of applications (due to not having to define languages from scratch), more objective evaluations of existing systems and challenges to the state of the art (due to the increases in expressiveness). PDDL is not yet expressive enough for some applications—in particular those that are better modeled as state vectors to support quick, contextual decisions about action and those requiring a hierarchical model from strategic to tactical. Several new languages have emerged and been adopted by different groups to also support these needs.

Second, the International Planning Competition has pressured the community to significantly improve the efficiency and representational capabilities of the systems by setting increasing challenges and requiring participants to make their code public (ICAPS 2012). The competition has expanded over the years to include tracks in uncertainty, learning and knowledge engineering.

Driven in part by the competitions and by advances in AI search algorithms, planning systems are now able to solve to (near) optimality problems that require plans with thousands of actions. Smarter data structures and more principled algorithms and heuristics have significantly expanded the scope of plan generation.

Third, as more researchers have made the transition to industrial laboratories, the range of applications has significantly expanded. Some were listed previously, but others include better manufacturing, elevator control, industrial copier management, managing web services, personalized e-learning and computer security.

Finally, to expedite development, two supportive technologies are being investigated: mixed initiative systems and knowledge engineering tools. Mixed initiative systems allow the user to be involved in the decision process by guiding the search, selecting from alternative plans, making changes to proposed solutions or interceding when something goes wrong. Knowledge

---

[26] Drew McDermott (ed.) 1998 The Planning Domain Definition Language Manual. Yale Computer Science Report 1165

[27] S. Edelkamp, J. Hoffmann. 2003. Taming numbers and durations in the model checking integrated planning system. Journal of Artificial Research. 20: 195-238.

[28] Gerevini, A., and Long, D. 2006. Plan constraints and preferences in PDDL3. In Proc. Int. Conference on Automated Planning and Scheduling (ICAPS- 2006) – International Planning Competition, 7–13

[29] Younes, Hakan L.S. and Michael L. Littmann. 2004. PPDDL 1.0: An Extension to PDDL for Expressing Planning Domains with Probabilistic Effects. Carnegie Mellon University, School of Computer Science. http://reports-archive.adm.cs.cmu.edu/anon/anon/home/ftp/2004/CMU-CS-04-167.pdf.

engineering tools support translation and verification of application-specific representational formats, such as web service, business modeling, software requirements and e-learning languages.

3.4.2.2. Gaps

The most nascent area of planning is mixed initiative/knowledge engineering. As new applications are investigated, it is becoming clear that objectives cannot always be stated precisely enough to admit optimization and that the humans who take part in the unfolding plan have opinions about how it should be. Additionally, the users don't want to modify the PDDL representation to make the planner produce a different answer. One key to autonomy is knowing when and how best to deploy it to maximize the efficacy of the human-computer system and to ensure trust. The key open question is: how does one develop a planner that best complements the automated system and the user's richer knowledge? This leads to issues of what information to provide, how to identify points in the plan generation and execution process, when the user can be most helpful, how to support development of new applications, how to explain the reasoning and how and when to present alternatives so that the user can make appropriate changes.

A related area is execution monitoring/replanning. Traditionally, plans were developed and then handed off for execution. However, to rely on a famous quote, "no battle plan survives contact with the enemy." Thus, monitoring the state of the world as the plan unfolds, detecting mismatches (either failures or opportunities) and adjusting the plan to accommodate (replan) is critical to successful action. The open issues are: what and how to monitor within the physical and computational constraints of the system, when to autonomously replan, when to refer back to the user and whether to use different objectives (e.g., stability, which means minimizing the changes to the existing plan) when replanning.

Finally, additional extensions to representations are needed to connect richer, domain specific representations to generalized planning representations. The representations must also allow users to articulate more complex goals/optimization objectives, to query progress and to define the bounds of execution.

3.4.3. Learning

Machine Learning has become one of the most effective approaches to developing intelligent, autonomous systems. Automatically inducing knowledge from data has generally been found to be more effective than manual knowledge engineering.[30] Development of state-of-the-art systems in computer vision,[31] robotics, natural language processing[32] and planning[33] now rely

---

[30] A. Blum and T. Mitchell, Proceedings of the 1998 Conference on Computational Learning Theory, July 1998; Combining Labeled and Unlabeled Data with Co-Training,"

[31] Sebe, Nicu, Ira Cohen, Ashutosh Garg, and Thomas S. Huang. 2005. Machine Learning in Computer Vision. Dordrecht: Springer.

[32] Jurafsky, Daniel, James H. Martin. 2008. An Introduction to Natural Language Processing, Computational Linguistics, and Speech Recognition Second Edition.

extensively on automated learning from training data. Mining large amounts of real-world data to find reliable patterns, generally results in more accurate and robust autonomous systems than manual software engineering. This also allows a system to automatically adapt to novel environments from actual experience operating in these situations.

3.4.3.1. State of the Art

The state of the art described below highlights the missed opportunities to apply proven techniques in learning for navigation and recognition to UxVs in order to improve general robustness, to reduce the volume of data that needs to be reviewed by human analysts and to reduce the false alarm rate.

Existing commercial UxVs are developed almost exclusively using manual software engineering and have little ability to learn and adapt to complex novel environments. However, robotics research has clearly illustrated the advantages of learning in developing robust and effective systems. The leading systems in the DARPA Grand Challenge and the Urban Challenge for autonomous UGVs all relied extensively on machine learning. There is a large body of well-developed learning techniques for autonomous UGV navigation that have demonstrated success in the DARPA Challenges as well as other DARPA robotics programs such as LAGR and Off-Road Autonomy (UPI).

There is also a large body of well-developed learning techniques for computer vision and perception. There are well developed learning methods for object, person and activity recognition,[34] such as technology developed in the DARPA Mind's Eye and Video and Image Retrieval and Analysis Tool (VIRAT) programs. These proven techniques need to be transferred to commercial systems.

3.4.3.2. Gaps

Most use of learning for autonomous navigation has been applied to ground vehicles and robots. Adaptive navigation approaches for air and marine vehicles are much less well developed. One important area for future development is to refine the existing learning methods for effective use in these alternative domains. Also, existing techniques for adaptive navigation have been developed for either unstructured but static environments (such as the desert-crossing task in the original DARPA Challenge) or dynamic but structured environments (such as the city navigation environment in the Urban Challenge). However, most UxVs are required to operate in environments that are *both* unstructured and dynamic, where existing maps provide little guidance and both cooperative and hostile agents abound. Developing learning methods that can cope with such complex environments is an important challenge for future R&D.

---

[33] Helmert, M.; Röger, G.; and Karpas, E. 2011. Fast Downward Stone Soup: A baseline for building planner portfolios. In Proceedings of the ICAPS-2011 Workshop on Planning and Learning (PAL), 28–35.
[34] Sebe, Nicu, Ira Cohen, Ashutosh Garg, and Thomas S. Huang. 2005. Machine Learning in Computer Vision. Dordrecht: Springer.

One of the primary limitations of most current machine-learning methods is that they require significant supervised training data. Building the requisite training data involves an expensive and laborious process in which human experts must label a large number of examples, e.g., annotate images with object labels or videos with activity labels. A number of techniques exist for reducing the amount of supervision that learning systems require. These include:

- Active Learning: The amount of supervision required is reduced by automatically selecting only those examples for labeling that will most improve the overall system performance.[35]
- Transfer Learning: Learning for a new "target" problem is aided by using knowledge previously acquired for related "source" problems.[36]
- Semi-Supervised Learning: A mix of labeled and unlabeled data is used to learn accurate knowledge with a limited amount of supervision.[37]
- Cross-modal training: One sensory modality is used to automatically train another; for example, LADAR information acquired at short range can be used to train visual interpretation from a much longer range (DARPA UPI program).
- Additional basic research on these and other approaches to reducing supervision in machine learning would decrease the time and expense needed to develop autonomous systems.

Another approach to minimizing supervision for training robots is *reinforcement learning*,[38] which only requires rewarding an agent at the successful completion of a complex multi-step task. However, learning from such delayed feedback generally requires a very large number of training experiences, which is not practical for real robots. Still another promising approach to reducing training time for learning multi-step tasks is *imitation learning*,[39] in which a system observes a human perform the task (possibly through teleoperation) and learns and generalizes from this experience. The successful use of imitation learning for controlling a model helicopter is a well-known research result.[40] Other approaches to reducing the training time of reinforcement learning are transfer learning, interactive reward shaping and advice-taking.[41] Additional basic research on these and other approaches to improving learning of complex, multi-step tasks would expedite the development of autonomous systems.

---

[35] Settles, Burr. 2011. Closing the Loop: Fast, Interactive Semi-Supervised Annotation with Queries on Features and Instances. EMNLP '11 Proceedings of the Conference on Empirical Methods in Natural Language Processing: 1467-1478.

[36] Pan, S. J. and Yang, Q., 2008. "A survey on transfer learning," http://www.cse.ust.hk/~sinnopan/publications/TLsurvey_0822.pdf.

[37] Chapelle, O., B. Scholkopf, A. Zien. 2006. Semi-Supervised Learning. MIT press.

[38] Sutton, Richard S. 1998. Reinforcement Learning. Cambridge, MA: MIT Press.

[39] Boularias, Abdeslam, Jens Kober, Jan Peters. 2011. Relative Entropy Inverse Reinforcement Learning. Proceedings of the 14th International Conference on Artificial Intelligence and Statistics

[40] Adam Coates, Pieter Abbeel, and Andrew Y. Ng. 2008. Learning for control from multiple demonstrations. In Proceedings of the 25th international conference on Machine learning, pages 144{151.

[41] Knox, Bradley, Peter Stone. 2011. Reinforcement Learning from Simultaneous Human and MDP Reward

Machine learning is generally effective at identifying specific categories of objects, people and activities for which it has been explicitly trained. However, many applications in autonomous systems, particularly in situational awareness and monitoring, require detecting unusual objects or events that may be malicious. Anomaly detection systems[42] attempt to identify such outliers; however, it is difficult to achieve high detection rates without also generating an unacceptable number of false-positive alarms. Fundamental research in anomaly detection is needed to support the eventual development of reliable autonomous monitoring systems.

3.4.4. Human-Robot Interaction/Human-System Interaction

Human-robot interaction (HRI) is a relatively new, multi-disciplinary field that addresses how people work or play with robots versus computers or tools. This is a subset of the larger field of human-system interaction, as the focus is on bi-directional, cognitive interactions in which the robot is a physically situated agent operating at a distance from the user, versus a computer or autopilot, thus leading to significant distinctions. In order to be consistent with the scientific literature, the term HRI will be used generally, but UxV will serve to describe the specific form of robot.

UxVs are distinctly different from computers, given that they are physically situated agents with impact in the physical world and often some degree of autonomy. UxVs are more capable than tools and may be delegated work or allowed bounded initiative. As embodied agents, robots elicit subconscious expectations of competence, adaptability, shared goals and interpersonal etiquette; these human expectations are dubbed "social responses" even though the human and robot may not be in a companionable relationship. HRI addresses six basic research issues: how humans and UxVs communicate; how to model the relationship between humans and UxVs for work, entertainment or causal interactions; how to study and enhance human-UxV teamwork; how to predict usability and reliability in the human-UxV team; how to capture and express the human-UxV interactions for a particular application domain; and how to characterize end-users.[43] As a result of this broad research scope, HRI spans unmanned systems, human factors, psychology, cognitive science, communication, human computer interaction, computer supported work groups and sociology. This large multi-disciplinary mix presents a very different mindset from traditional engineering design, interface development or ergonomics.

The benefits to DoD on focusing on the human-machine system versus the platform are: improved performance, reduced cost of operating and designing platforms, increased adaptability of existing systems to new situations and accelerated adoption. Better human-UxV teamwork leads to faster performance of tasks with fewer errors. Better teamwork, improved communication interfaces and improved usability and reliability for applications reduce the number of humans needed to operate the system. They also reduce the cost of designing

---

[42] Chandola, Varun, Arindam Banerjee, Vipin Kumar. 2009. Anomaly Detection: A Survey. ACM Computing Surveys.

[43] Burke, J.L., et al., Final report for the DARPA/NSF interdisciplinary study on human-robot interaction. Systems, Man, and Cybernetics, Part C: Applications and Reviews, IEEE Transactions on, 2004. 34(2): p. 103-112.

unique displays for different systems or redesigning unmanned systems with poor HRI support by "getting the design right the first time." Better understanding of the roles and limitations of humans, UxVs and autonomous capabilities in a particular situation help design systems that can not only monitor for violations of limitation but also begin to project new needs and demands—therefore increasing adaptability. Better HRI increases both the fitness of an unmanned system for accomplishing missions and human trust that the system is reliable; these factors are expected to accelerate adoption. Advanced HRI ethnographic methods can also help identify spontaneous innovations in the use of unmanned systems, speeding adoption of new capabilities, uses and best practices.

The two teamwork styles with a robot are *remote presence* and *taskable agency*. In most DoD applications, the goal of the system is to extend the reach of the warfighter into denied areas, thus characterizations based on type of teamwork within a joint cognitive system are more useful for conceptualizing HRI issues than the more general taxonomies based on personal proximity to the robot.

Remote presence means that the human works through the unmanned system to perceive and act in real-time at a distance. In remote presence teams, the human wants to stay in the loop not just because of limitations of computer vision but also for opportunities to see the unmodeled or the unexpected. However, the human does not necessarily need to be a robot operator in order to work in distal environments. Team performance depends on the unmanned system helping humans to 1) compensate for impaired sense making due to working through the robot (e.g., the robot mediates the environment, thus reducing information) and 2) minimize the distracting workload of directly controlling the robot.

Taskable agents means that the unmanned system is delegated sole responsibility for the mission. In taskable agent teams, the human hands-off a mission and attends to other missions until the unmanned system returns. In taskable agency, the human and robot are more loosely coupled than in remote presence teams, but they still must interact to ensure correct delegation, to confirm that the intent was completely communicated and to cognitively integrate findings when the unmanned system returns. Trust is a major factor in the adoption of taskable agents.

The choice of team style should depend on the mission. Remote presence is distinct from taskable agency. However, different missions require different strategies. Covert surveillance may require an unmanned system to work independently for days or weeks before returning with valuable data, while a Special Forces mission may require unmanned systems to enable constant situation over watch.

Many approaches to unmanned systems consider remote presence to be teleoperation; the human is in the loop only due to deficits in autonomous capabilities. Indeed, the Task Force saw indications that unmanned systems were viewed as either fully autonomous or totally teleoperated. This "all or nothing" false dichotomy ignores helpful autonomous capabilities such as guarded motion, waypoint navigation and perceptual cueing that, if correctly implemented, can reduce workload on the operators and allow them to focus on the mission.

3.4.4.1. State of the Art

The state of the art is that there is a solid base of knowledge that is widely underutilized in UxV systems. The benefits of using established human-centered design principles and resulting system design, interfaces and protocols are reduced manpower, lower human workload, better performance, fewer errors and greater user acceptance.

Categorizing the state of the art in HRI for unmanned systems is challenging because HRI research is dominated by research into assistive and entertainment robots, not robots which perform cognitive work with or for humans. The one exception to this is the rise of robot telecommunicating surrogates; however, these systems generally provide mobile video conferencing rather than performing the type of perception and actions needed by the warfighter. Beyond the six key areas of interest, determining the human:robot ratio and robot ethics are relevant HRI issues for the DoD.

Progress is being made in three of the six key areas. Methods for communicating with unmanned systems continue to improve, with advances in natural language (see Section 3.14 below) and higher resolution display technology. However, communication of the system state, or the visibility of what the robot is doing and why, to improve trust remains an open question. Multi-modal displays are being actively researched to combat the tendency to overload an operator's visual channel by displaying all information on the operator control unit screen. Modeling the relationship between humans and robots for accomplishing a task is still in its infancy. It is not known how to represent differences in human and robot capabilities, and the ramifications of using one agent instead of another are not understood.

Research in human-robot teams appears to be largely duplicating human-human team research and, not unexpectedly, shows that humans expect unmanned systems to meet expectations of a team member with known competences.[44] A major challenge is how increase the capability of an unmanned system to provide *mutual predictability* (who is doing what and when), *directability* (both to specify objectives but also how to adapt to the unexpected) and *common ground* (including special languages or protocols to ensure that the human and robot are sharing the same goals and information).

HRI has made less progress on informing design. HRI studies have largely been descriptive rather than proscriptive; the best source of literature on how predict the usability and reliability in a human-robot team is from the larger cognitive systems literature which views robots as just

---

[44] Klein, G., et al. 2004. Ten challenges for making automation a "team player" in joint human-agent activity. Intelligent Systems, IEEE. 19(6): p. 91-95.

one type of cognitive agent.[45] Likewise, representing applications and end-users and what that means for the design of reliable HRI has produced only initial taxonomies; this remains an underdeveloped area of HRI.

One major area of concern in unmanned systems is the appropriate human:robot ratio, which remains greater than 1.0. HRI research views the appropriate human:robot ratio as the interplay of the six key areas of HRI (communication, modeling, teamwork, usability and reliability, task domains and characteristics of the users). This systems-level perspective suggests the ratio depends on the design of the system, including the competence and reliability of the robot, the mission, the type of interface and consequences of failure. The minimum operator level for most unmanned systems appears to be two people per platform, with one person to operate the platform and the other to look at the incoming data or to protect the operator. While platform-centric programs, such as the DARPA Unmanned Combat Aircraft Vehicle (UCAV) program, have demonstrated a single operator controlling four platforms under nominal conditions, these programs have not explored what happens when there are significant vehicle failures or the situation suddenly changes. This presents the human out-of-the-loop (OOTL) control problem, where an operator who is primarily focused on another task has to suddenly identify and rectify a fault.[46] In general, the more focused the operator is on the other task (i.e., the more out of the loop) the harder it is for that individual to respond effectively.

The attempts to reduce the human:robot ratio without considering the principles of HRI appear to be a form of the Air Traffic Control Metaphor Fallacy.[47] The air traffic controller (ATC) metaphor is as follows: UAVs will become sufficiently autonomous such that a single person can manage multiple platforms in the same manner as an air traffic controller manages flights within a region, and since an ATC can handle multiple aircraft safely, a single human will be able to handle multiple platforms safely. The ATC metaphor is fallacious because it ignores the pilot-in-command role, which is unique to unmanned vehicles. If a manned air vehicle encounters difficulties, the ATC does not assume control of the aircraft; the pilot on board remains in charge of each individual aircraft and responds to the local problem. In unmanned systems, the operator is expected to be the de facto pilot-in-command of each vehicle and to take over operations in case of a problem. In terms of perceptual viewpoints, the human is expected to go from a broad, external view of ``dots on a screen" to directly operating the platform in a degraded and possibly unknown state.

---

[45] Woods, D. and E. Hollnagel. 2006. Joint Cognitive Systems: Patterns in Cognitive Systems Engineering. Boca Raton, FL: CRC Press, Taylor and Francis.

[46] Kaber, D.B. and M.R. Endsley. 1997. Out-of-the-loop performance problems and the use of intermediate levels of automation for improved control system functioning and safety. Process Safety Progress. 16(3): p. 126-131.

[47] Murphy, R.R. and J.L. Burke. 2010. The Safe Human-Robot Ratio (Chapter 3), in Human-Robot Interactions in Future Military Operations, F.J. M. Barnes, Editor Ashgate. p. 31-49.

An area of HRI that has received significant attention is *robot ethics,*[48] and while theoretically interesting, this debate on *functional* morality has had unfortunate consequences. It increases distrust and acceptance of unmanned systems because it implies that robots will not act with bounded rationality and that autonomy is equivalent to high degrees of initiative. Treating unmanned systems as if they had sufficient independent agency to reason about morality distracts from designing appropriate rules of engagement and ensuring *operational morality.* Operational morality is concerned with the professional ethics in design, deployment and handling of robots. Many companies and program managers appear to treat autonomy as exempt from operational responsibilities. While aspects of an autonomous capability may be non-deterministic, this does not relieve designers of the responsibility of designing from resilience in the face of the "expected unpredictable."[49]

3.4.4.2. Gaps

The immediate gaps in HRI for unmanned systems fall into two related categories: *natural user interfaces enabling trusted human-system collaboration* and *understandable autonomous system behaviors.* These categories reflect the effort to enable the warfighter to achieve reach into a distal environment. As unmanned systems become more integrated with peace-keeping operations and work beside soldiers (for example, providing transportation and logistics support) or directly assist them (e.g., use of robots for casualty evacuation), these issues will become more important. As seen by the distribution of papers in the Association for Computing Machinery (ACM)/IEEE Conference on Human-Robot Interaction, HRI for assistive and entertainment robots is being actively researched with significantly less attention to HRI for unmanned systems. HRI research for unmanned systems will require dedicated funding initiatives.

Natural user interfaces and trusted human-system collaboration bring together the threads of communication and teamwork research to leverage best human and machine capabilities. The gaps in this category are:

- Operator control interfaces that support rapid training on systems with many degrees of freedom and usual sensors and viewpoints, as well as transitioning from novice functionality to expertise.
- Perceptually oriented interfaces and sensor placement designed around the psycho-physical attributes of the human perceptual system.
- Interfaces that provide visibility of what the unmanned system(s) is doing and why relative to the mission objectives.
- Effective human-system dialog using natural human interaction modes, especially natural language and gestures.

---

[48] Arkin, R.C., Governing Lethal Behavior in Autonomous Robots2009: Chapman and Hall/CRC Press.
[49] Murphy, R.R. and D.D. Woods. 2009. Beyond Asimov: The Three Laws of Responsible Robotics. IEEE Intelligent Systems. 24(4): p. 14-20

Predictable and understandable autonomous system behaviors rely on advances in modeling, specification and data collection. The major gaps are:

- Prescriptive models of HRI in unmanned systems that can be used to create design criteria, evaluation standards and operational test and evaluation procedures.
- Models of what operators or decision makers need to know about the system or state in order to maintain trust in the predictable outcomes from using the system.
- Cost effective data collection and analysis methods for understanding how unmanned systems are being used in the field and for what situations autonomous capabilities are being used.

3.4.5. Natural Language

Natural language processing (NLP) concerns the development of computing systems that can communicate with people using ordinary human languages such as English (Jurafsky & Martin, 2008). *Automated speech recognition* (ASR) translates a speech signal into text, and *natural language understanding* (NLU) translates this text into a formal representation of its meaning that a computer can manipulate. Natural language is related to human-robot interaction, as giving an unmanned system imprecise verbal directives would simplify and speed up delegation. However, natural language is a separate research discipline and is considered separately here.

Natural language is the most normal and intuitive way for humans to instruct autonomous systems; it allows them to provide diverse, high-level goals and strategies rather than detailed teleoperation. However, understanding human language is difficult since it is inherently ambiguous, and context must be used to infer the intended meaning. Therefore, building autonomous systems that can follow English instructions as well as human speech is a very difficult technical challenge. Therefore, traditional *graphical user interfaces* (GUIs) are frequently a more effective approach to communicating with computing systems. However, in many situations (e.g., when the user's hands are otherwise engaged), language is a very desirable mode of communication.

3.4.5.1. State of the Art

The state of the art highlights the missed opportunities for both operators and dismounted forces, within the bounds of visual attention, to operate UxVs in a heads up, hands free mode. This would reduce workload and increase soldier survivability in hostile environments.

To our knowledge, no existing UxV system accepts natural language instruction. Existing ASR and NLU technology can only support simple language instruction in which a limited vocabulary and small set of commands is not sufficient for the demands of the task. Apple's SIRI system for requesting information on the iPhone (based partly on results from DARPA's Cognitive Assistant that Learns to Organize (CALO) project), and Microsoft's SYNC system for controlling automobile mobile phone and entertainment systems are examples of the commercial state-of-the art in natural-language technology. Such technology could be adapted to provide simple natural-language interfaces for autonomous systems.

3.4.5.2. Gaps

Developing more capable NLP for autonomous systems requires additional R&D. Existing NLU is largely focused on understanding written text, rather than instructions and dialog that concern direct interaction with the world. Basic research is needed to develop more user-friendly autonomous systems that can effectively communicate using human language.

In particular, the following problems require additional fundamental research:

- Grounded language interpretation: Connecting words and phrases to the perception of objects and events in the world, e.g. (Roy et al., 2002).
- Understanding instructional language: Mapping natural-language instructions to formal action sequences that a robot can execute, e.g. (Tellex et al., 2011).
- Understanding spatial language: Interpreting linguistic expressions that refer to spatial relationships in the environment, e.g. (Skubic et al., 2004).
- Situated dialog: Mixed-initiative natural language dialog for human-robot interaction and collaboration (Bohus et al., 2011).

3.4.6. Multi-Agent Coordination

Multi-agent coordination is a term that is broadly applied to accomplishing a task that is distributed over multiple robots, software agents or humans. Each agent is considered to have some degree of individual autonomy, and the coordination may either emerge from the agents interacting or negotiating with each other directly (distributed coordination) or be explicitly directed by a planner (centralized coordination). Regardless of the coordination scheme, the distribution of an activity across multiple agents implies that coordination schemes must address synchronization of the agents with each other and to dynamically changing aspects of the environment or mission. Synchronization is often, but not universally, referred to as cooperation by multi-agent systems researchers, with cooperation being either active (such as in robot soccer) or non-active (such as the foraging behavior seen in ants). Collaboration is related to cooperation but is treated as a distinct topic as it assumes that the agents have a cognitive understanding of each other's capabilities, can monitor progress towards the goal, and engage in more human-like teamwork. Multi-agent coordination and human-robot interaction are related fields of inquiry, but in general, multi-agent coordination research focuses more on cooperation schemes for different types of configurations of distributed agents and human-robot interaction focuses more on cognition in collaboration. This subsection will limit discussion to cooperation in multi-robot systems, which is a subset of multi-agent coordination.

Coordination of multiple UxVs offers at least four benefits: increased coverage, decreased costs, redundancy and specialization. Multiple UxVs can provide shared, persistent coverage over wider areas than a single platform, providing sensor coverage while acting as network repeaters. Many low-cost UxVs can provide a viable alternative to a single high-cost low-observable platform or to having to create highly protected systems for counter anti-access, area denial environments. Multiple low cost platforms used in parallel offer redundancy in the presence of noise, clutter, jamming and attempts at camouflage, concealment and deception: even if several are lost or distracted, some will succeed. Multiple specialized, or heterogeneous, platforms offer reduced costs and design requirements. For example, within a heterogeneous team one specialized UxV may refuel other UxVs, simplifying both design and platform costs.

Autonomous coordination amplifies the benefits of multiple UxVs performing coordination faster, optimally and with fewer errors than a human and reducing or eliminating dependencies on network communication or other resources. Autonomous planning capabilities can optimize UxVs with dynamically changing constraints, for example the allocation of limited resources such as radiofrequency (RF) spectrum while handling airspace deconfliction. Unlike a human, planning and scheduling algorithms can keep up with thousands of agents and constraints in real-time. Coordination is not limited to motion planning for parallel activities, but it includes coordinating serial activities, such as a general purpose UxV tasking a specialized UxV to obtain confirmatory observations from a different spectrum or viewpoint (e.g. air-ground). Autonomous coordination does not always require network communication, allowing UxVs to be used in covert, spoofed or communications-denied regions.

3.4.6.1. State of the Art
The state of the art highlights missed opportunities to deploy swarms of low cost UxVs, to efficiently and effectively coordinate UGV/UAV teams, or for a UxV to opportunistically take advantage of the resources from a nearby UxV operating independently.

In multi-robot system research, UxV teams are typically described in terms of their coordination scheme and overall system attributes, following the taxonomy synthesized from a review of existing research. The coordination scheme captures the organization (strongly centralized, weakly centralized or distributed), coordination methods (strongly, weakly or not), a UxVs knowledge of its team members (aware or unaware) and cooperation (explicit or implicit). The system attributes are the presence and amount of communication, team composition (homogeneous or heterogeneous), underlying cognitive systems architecture (behavioral, deliberative or hybrid) and team size.

Unaware systems are those in which the UxV does not know of the presence of other UxVs. These systems are biologically inspired by ant colonies, E. coli, etc. Researchers have pushed these models in simulation with hundreds to thousands of robots for foraging and surveillance tasks. Unaware systems can perform more complex tasks such as transporting objects, as each robot can sense the object and independently move the object towards the goal. Another example of unaware systems are "self-healing" mine fields or unattended sensors. Unaware algorithms are well-suited for swarms or colonies of low-cost, homogeneous UxVs with simple behaviors in communication-denied environments.

Aware but weakly coordinated systems are those in which a robot may sense the presence of other UxVs but does not explicitly communicate intentions or plans with others. For example, in a weakly coordinated team, a UxV may follow its team members by determining their average direction of motion. In the DARPA Urban Grand Challenge, the autonomous cars could recognize other cars but had to infer the others' intent and predict their actions. Weakly coordinated schemes usually avoid the need for network communication by endowing individual UxVs with a set of expectations, policies, or rules of engagement and sufficient sensing to be aware of other UxVs. The DARPA Urban Grand Challenge illustrates that the robots can coordinate with each other without being a collaborative team or working on a common objective. Other examples of aware but weakly coordinated systems include the DARPA Software for Distributed Robots (SDR) program that demonstrated 100 small UGVs working together (CentiBots), the DARPA LANdroids program that demonstrated 10 small UGVs maintaining a mobile ad hoc network indoors and the proposed 60 small UGV Swarmanoid project funded by the European Commission.

Strongly coordinated, distributed systems are a very active area of research, especially with the advances emerging from the international RoboCup robot soccer competition and auction-based task allocation schemes. Robot soccer is an exemplar of a robot system in which individuals in heterogeneous roles must be tightly coordinated to accomplish the objective in a dynamically changing environment. Some leagues permit network communications between UGVs on a team but many entries now have UGVs that subtly signal their intent to their teammates or learn the tendencies of their partners to overcome network or computational latencies. Auction-based schemes and combinatorial optimization methods grew out of the contract net protocol[50] and have become the de facto standard in distributed groups of UxVs determining task assignments or resource allocation without a centralized arbiter. In contract net protocols, UxVs offer bids on their availability and suitability for a task or need for a resource. Contract net protocols incur a high network communication cost.

Strongly-coordinated centralized systems in which team members are directed by a central controller, and continually share information about intent and actions, are a topic of research, but in general, researchers eschew centralized control because of the dependence on a single agent and communications to that agent. The recent focus on centralized systems has been on selecting one of the team members to serve as the leader rather than having a dedicated, off-site agent serving as the central authority. This moves communication to a local network rather than requiring network connectivity to a remote server agent that must persist throughout the team's operation and ensures that there is no single point of failure.

Distributed and centralized systems use a variety of cognitive systems architectures. Individual robots in distributed systems are usually either implemented with a general core behavioral or hybrid deliberative/reactive architecture with social rules or protocols added as needed to

---

[50] Gerkey, B.P. and M.J. Mataric. 2002. Sold!: auction methods for multirobot coordination. Robotics and Automation, IEEE Transactions on. 18(5): p. 758-768

adapt to the level of coordination and communication. Centralized systems often rely on top-down hierarchical multi-agent planning systems. These types of systems include the National Institute of Standards and Technology's (NIST) Real-time Control Systems (4D/RCS), Draper Laboratory's All-Domain Execution and Planning Technology (ADEPT) and Maritime Open Architecture Autonomy (MOAA) and NASA Jet Propulsion Laboratory's (JPL) Continuous Activity Scheduling Planning Execution and Replanning (CASPER) autonomy software architectures.

3.4.6.2. Gaps

Gaps between the state of the art of autonomy for multi-agent coordination and implementation reflect both the newness of the field and barriers preventing transferrable research. The primary barrier to research with relevant results is the reliance on simulations due to the costs of capable UxVs and experimentation and the time required to conduct field trials. However, the lack of compelling applications to drive the research also hinder researchers producing results on scenarios with more readily apparent value to the DoD.

The major gaps requiring additional research to enable the Department of Defense to realize the benefits of autonomy for multiple UxVs are a lack of:

- *Formal mapping of appropriate coordination scheme and system attributes for a specific type of mission.* To date, the design of multi-agent systems has been ad hoc, with research focused on developing new coordination algorithms. Less emphasis has been placed on new application development or on consolidating research results into a formal, proscriptive design theory that would allow a designer to select the most appropriate system for a particular mission. While current taxonomies provide initial steps in this direction, this topic requires dedicated effort.
- *Provably correct emergent behavior.* Unaware and aware, weakly coordinated systems take advantage of biologically inspired algorithms that minimize communication, computation and often sensing. These are desirable attributes for low-cost swarms; however, there are currently no tools to predict that the desired correct behavior will emerge or what will happen if the environment changes radically.
- *Interference and opportunistic re-tasking.* Having more robots work on a shared objective increases the possibility that individual robots will unintentionally interfere with each other, reducing effectiveness. More importantly, the possibility of many UxVs working locally as part of one system but globally as another, often spatially co-located, introduces opportunities for real-time sharing or allocation of capabilities.
- *Communication.* Communication includes both how and what to communicate. Many biological systems such as flocks, swarms and herds communicate implicitly through posture, proxemics, noises, color and pheromones. An open question remains as to the reliability of implicit communication for UxV applications and even, if possible, the tradeoffs with explicit communication. The content of explicit communication between UxVs is also an open question, especially when UxVs should (if at all) use a shared, synchronized common relevant operating picture, which may consume bandwidth and computational resources. Regardless of the content of explicit communication between

UxVs or a centralized server, robust network communication is essential for strongly and most weakly coordinated systems.

It should be noted that multi-agent system research has typically found that effective coordination requires the individual UxVs to have at least some modicum of onboard intelligence. Effective and robust coordination of multiple UxVs may not be possible without increased onboard autonomy.

3.5. Technical Recommendations

The future development of autonomy requires a new paradigm; one that preserves a rapid, innovative development cycle influenced by the interaction between operators and developers, as witnessed during the recent conflicts in Iraq and Afghanistan. DoD should leverage lessons learned through the use of current systems to create operationally-relevant challenge problems for the R&D community.

The objective should be to create a technology base of diverse, platform-independent, transparent *cognitive functions* and *tactics* for integration into new missions. The Task Force sees this as an iterative process. First, DoD should aim to formalize a set of human-centric principles, such as design trade spaces, costs of coordination, etc. into a set of questions to be applied at the beginning of, and throughout, the design process. Second, demonstration tiger teams should be formed from academia, government/not-for-profit labs and industry to focus on active experimentation challenges. Active experimentation should explore likely scenarios and desired mission capabilities (e.g., China, rogue states, etc.) in order to discover new, unpredicted missions, especially those which might be executing using small, inexpensive UxVs, which seem likely to be used by adversaries—both nation states and asymmetric actors.

Based on its review, the **Task Force makes the following recommendations:**

- DoD should abandon efforts to define levels of autonomy and develop an autonomous system reference framework that:
    - Focuses on how autonomy supports specific capabilities.
    - Identifies cognitive functional responsibilities to be delegated to the human or the computer, either by the needs of a specific echelon or by phase in a mission timeline.
    - Makes visible the systems level trades of fitness, plans, impact, perspective and responsibility inherent in the design of autonomous capabilities.
- ASD(R&D) should work with the Military Services to develop a coordinated S&T program to strengthen key enabling autonomy technologies (perceptual processing, planning, learning, human-robot interaction, natural language understanding, and multi-agent coordination) with emphasis on:
    - Natural user interfaces and trusted human-system collaboration.
    - Perception and situational awareness to operate in a complex battle space.

- o Large-scale teaming of manned and unmanned systems.
- o Test and evaluation of autonomous systems.
- ASD(R&E) and the Services should stimulate the S&T program with challenge problems motivated by operational experience and evolving mission requirements
  - o Create focused on-site collaborations across academia, government/not-for-profit labs and industry to discover unpredicted uses of small, inexpensive UxVs by adversaries.
- The Department should broadly strengthen the government technical workforce for autonomy by attracting AI and software engineering experts and establishing career paths and promotion opportunities that will retain them.

4.0 Acquisition Issues of Autonomy

Because they provide a new capability with which operational experience is lacking, those desiring to acquire autonomous systems have had difficulty navigating the DoD requirements definition and acquisition processes. No unmanned, autonomous systems have formally completed operational test and evaluation prior to being released to the field. Rather, urgent needs have forced deployment of prototype or developmental systems before completing all acquisition milestones. The problems with DoD requirements and acquisition processes have been studied extensively by other DSB Task Forces,[51] so the current Task Force limited its investigation of acquisition issues to those that are uniquely associated with autonomous systems.

This chapter will discuss the key acquisition issues associated with autonomous systems in three sections focused on the requirements and development phase, test and evaluation and the transition to operational deployment, respectively.

4.1. Requirements and Development

Evolving requirements were discovered through operational experimentation. A lack of operational experience with autonomous systems has led to limited advocacy for autonomous systems within the Military Services' requirements processes. Most of the programmatic activity has been directed at technology and prototype platforms with a broad goal of demonstrating the value of these systems to the ISR mission. For this mission, it was believed that unmanned airborne platforms would provide data collection capabilities with better persistence and resolution than satellites and increased mission duration and safety when compared with manned aircraft. Since the initial focus was on unmanned, remotely operated systems, the design effort was primarily focused on platform issues, with secondary efforts focused on the operator control station. Only limited attention was paid to issues of autonomy.

The conflicts in Iraq and Afghanistan provided an operational pull for unmanned systems—particularly air and ground vehicles—that resulted in the deployment of many prototype or developmental systems. Once in theater, the demands of combat, combined with the ingenuity of the troops that operated the systems, resulted in unmanned systems being used extensively. This operational experimentation led to the employment of the systems in unanticipated ways with great benefits. The key missions that drove the evolution of unmanned systems were ISR, the defeat of improvised explosive devices and the pursuit and elimination of high value targets (HVTs).

---

[51] DSB Task Force on Improvements to Services Contracting, March 2011; DSB Task Force on Department of Defense Policies and Procedures for the Acquisition of Information Technology, March 2009; DSB Task Force on Creating a DoD Strategic Acquisition Platform, April 2009; DSB Task Force on Fulfillment of Urgent Operational Needs, July 2009.

Rapid development has led to both ground and air vehicles that have proven their value against IEDs. Ground systems were used both for convoy protection by traversing the route with an unmanned platform containing sensors to detect the presence of IEDs and for explosive ordnance disposal (EOD) by providing the EOD technicians the capability to disable devices while staying at a safe distance. The persistence of UAVs was critical for surveillance of convoy routes by enabling airborne detection of IEDs. UAVs also provided unwarned arrival of ISR sensors that often observed the adversaries placing the IED and followed them after they left the site. This latter capability was part of a campaign to defeat the entire IED network (including the bomb maker), which is a higher leverage activity than just focusing on detecting and neutralizing the devices.

The most important development for the HVT mission was arming UAVs, combining ISR and strike on the same platform to reduce the reaction time and shorten the kill chain. The fleeting, often without warning, window of opportunity against an HVT required both the long-term persistent observation provided by an ISR UAV enabling target confirmation and rapid strike without hand-off delays. This functionality was enabled by arming the platform. The operational concepts for most manned systems separated the ISR and strike functions. Consequently, the combination of strike and ISR on a single platform was essentially a revolutionary new capability.

Another critical capability for which requirements have evolved was the direct connectivity of airborne ISR platforms to ground platforms. This connectivity was achieved in two ways— through network communications with remote operators of primarily large platforms and through deployment of small platforms under direct operational control of forward deployed forces. The improved situational awareness provided by being able to "see over the next hill" and to have a real-time, larger-scale context of dynamic combat scenarios improved effectiveness and saved lives.

The impact of this direct connectivity stimulated a number of quick-reaction development programs to enhance capability, largely through improved sensors, and to increase capacity by rapidly producing and deploying additional units. As a result, the number and scope of unmanned assets has increased dramatically. However, one of the unintended consequences of this rapid expansion of unmanned systems is that they require significant manpower for operations and support. Figure 4-1 illustrates the manning requirements for two important Air Force systems. The situation has evolved such that the Air Force has declared that its most critical staffing problem is *manning its unmanned platforms.*

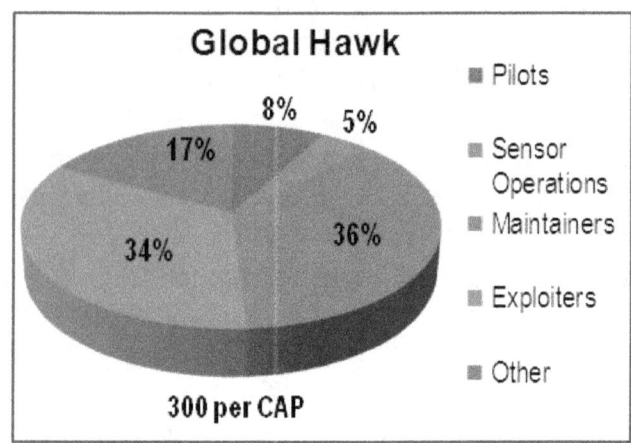
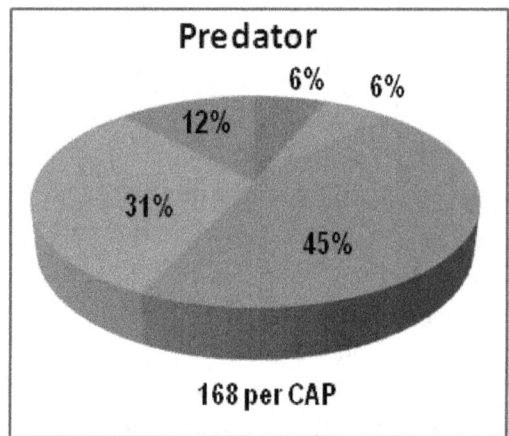

Figure 4-1 Manning Unmanned Platforms is a Key Staffing Problem

One of the reasons for the significant manning requirement for unmanned systems is that they were used in unintended ways. As discussed in Chapter 3, the experience with autonomous systems is that they are often brittle when used in new ways and the traditional response has been to increase staffing to work around limitations. Further, since the development systems rushed to theater were originally designed as remotely operated platforms to demonstrate capability, little consideration was given to identifying and designing cognitive functions that could be delegated to the computer to reduce manpower.

As combat operations wind down, there is a need for the Joint Staff and the Military Services to capture the operational lessons learned associated with unmanned systems. Concepts of operations must be developed by the planners to integrate unmanned systems into future mission scenarios. The requirements process must recognize the proven value of these capabilities and ensure that they are factored into the specifications for new systems.

Autonomy provides the opportunity to expand capabilities, yet it poses unique acquisition challenges. There is significant potential for increased use of autonomy to have a dramatic impact on the manning requirements for unmanned systems. Manpower costs are a large part of the DoD budget and the fiscal constraints of the pending budget environment will provide a strong motivation to increase efficiencies and add capability to unmanned systems to free people for more critical purposes.

Using the Air Force staffing requirement for its remotely piloted aircraft combat air patrols (CAP) presented in Figure 4.1 as an example, possible ways autonomy can reduce manpower include:

■ *Piloting/sensor operation*: Currently, it takes multiple operators to manage the flight and sensor operation functions for both the Predator and Global Hawk systems. While it will be essential to maintain a "human in the loop" to supervise operations and to make critical decisions such as those related to weapons release, the effective use of autonomy technology will enable a single operator to manage multiple vehicles. This goal can be achieved by delegating decisions such as take-off and landing, waypoint navigation and sensor-enabled situational awareness to the computer.

■ *Maintenance*: Using autonomy for on-board equipment health and status monitoring should improve reliability and reduce the maintenance staff required to support operations.

■ *Exploitation*: About a third of the staff required to support Air Force UAVs are devoted to processing sensor data and exploiting them to create useful information. Even with this staffing level, the rapid growth in data volume is making it very difficult to keep up. There are many opportunities to use autonomy capability to increase the capacity of the intelligence analysts assigned to the exploitation function.

In exploring the use of increased autonomy for reducing manpower, the Task Force urges caution against falling into the "Substitution Myth" by trying to replace humans with autonomous systems without considering how machines change work patterns, responsibilities and training. As discussed in Chapter 3, this is one of the common misperceptions associated with autonomy and the proper way to think about the design of autonomous systems is to use the reference framework to address the allocation of cognitive functions between the human and the computer. In this context, autonomy complements the human and allows the human to perceive and act in remote environments. By leveraging the framework, it is also likely that autonomy upgrades will provide entirely new functions, extending the life and increasing the flexibility of existing platforms.

Unlike many defense systems, the critical capability provided by autonomy is embedded in the system software. Software, and therefore the autonomy capability, should be able to be upgraded more frequently, and at lower cost, than capability that is primarily embedded in hardware. Specifically, in the budget-constrained, post-conflict environment confronting the DoD, the unmanned systems currently in the inventory (especially the largest, most expensive platforms) will likely need to be used for a long time. Upgrading the software for these systems to increase autonomy provides the opportunity to reduce manpower and expands the ability to address new, evolving missions.

Software poses a special set of acquisition and development challenges, and, if well managed, opportunities that differ from those traditionally associated with hardware development. With the use of spiral development concepts, capability can be added incrementally at more frequent intervals than can be achieved in hardware. This characteristic provides the flexibility to react and adapt to changing and unanticipated requirements from new and evolving mission applications. However, achieving this flexibility requires the structure and architecture of the software system to be designed to enable it. Hardware-oriented development milestones do not focus on these issues so they often get overlooked. Many of the recommendations of the

DSB Task Force on Department of Defense Policies and Procedures for the Acquisition of Information Technology[52] will benefit software-intensive autonomous systems, including:

■ Adopting new acquisition policies modeled on successful commercial practices for rapid acquisition and continuous upgrade of information technology (IT) capabilities by using an agile process geared to developing meaningful increments of capability, prioritized on technical need, in 18 months or less.

■ Strengthening the technical expertise relative to software acquisition of the DoD workforce.

The autonomous systems framework developed in Chapter 3 will be very useful in the transition from mission requirements to design because it will encourage explicit decisions around the human supervision of, and collaboration with, the autonomous system. Further, it will provide an important context for developing the software architecture by supplying a structure for assessing the flexibility and growth in capability that the system should accommodate to support evolving requirements and new missions.

Because of the differing needs of hardware and software development, the Task Force encourages the Military Services to separate the acquisition of autonomous system software from the hardware platform. Experience has shown that, when these two developments are combined, important attention to critical autonomy design decisions often get lost due to focus on platform capability and the mismatch between hardware-specific acquisition milestones and effective software development.

While the autonomy software must operate seamlessly with the hardware platform, this requirement can be accommodated while separating software and hardware acquisition by having the autonomy program create a government-owned software package with an open architecture and published interfaces. This package can then be provided as government-furnished equipment to the platform developer. This software-first program strategy will keep the focus on the important capacity of autonomy technology to enable new capabilities. It will also allow the Department to take advantage of new technology by allowing any contractor, laboratory or government agency to modify or expand the system without having to go back to the original developer. As illustrated in Table 4-1, the Task Force reviewed a number of initiatives across the DoD and Military Services that are directed at creating government-owned, open software packages for various mission domains. The efforts should be accelerated and expanded.

Even if the autonomous system is acquired with a single integrated hardware/software procurement, the government program manager should, at a minimum, structure the contract

---

[52] DSB Task Force on Department of Defense Policies and Procedures for the Acquisition of Information Technology; March 2009.

Table 4-1 Representative DoD Autonomy Open Software Initiatives

Program	Key Characteristics
Office of the Secretary of Defense's (OSD) Unmanned Air Systems Open Architecture and Services Repository	▪ Formalizes open architecture based on modular open systems architecture (MOSA) principles ▪ Establishes a enterprise service repository to re-use and share unmanned systems capabilities across DoD ▪ Provides guidance on how to implement OA and share capabilities ▪ Defines approach to open competition for technology acquisition
Air Force Research Laboratory's Foxhunt Program	▪ Vehicle-agnostic control of UAVs cooperating in teams through cross-cueing of vehicle and sensor behaviors ▪ Industry-defined UAV C2 Initiative (UCI)-based interoperability protocols ▪ Flexible, open standards-based warfighter interface ▪ Foundation for autonomous decentralized mission execution
NUWC Open Architecture for Autonomy & Control of UUVs	▪ Moves beyond vehicle-centric, mission specific or proprietary approaches ▪ Provides unified autonomy design and module re-use ▪ Encourages and controls incremental improvements ▪ Government owns and controls the code base. Industry gets paid to develop
SPAWAR Multi-Robot Operator Control Unit (MOCU)	▪ Control multiple heterogeneous vehicles ▪ Vehicle and protocol type independent ▪ Modular and scalable; flexible user interface; 3D graphics ▪ Enables 3rd party development ▪ In use as the common Operator Control Unit (OCU) for the Littoral Combat Ship (LCS) USV mission modules ▪ Planned for use in Navy's Advanced EOD Robotic Systems (AEODRS) program
Army's Unmanned Systems (Air, Ground and Maritime) Initial Capabilities Document	▪ Provides an overarching and unifying strategy for the development of interoperable unmanned systems across the domains ▪ Initial focus on common operator control systems for small UAVs ▪ Integration of intelligent analytics for persistent surveillance systems

to acquire full government ownership of the autonomy, including source code and all documentation required for a third party to be able to upgrade the functional capability. Because this approach has not been adopted on many of the currently deployed systems, the government is constrained to working only with the original development contractor when upgrading or expanding capability. In the budget-constrained environment confronting the DoD, it may be a good long-term investment for the Military Services to negotiate with the prime contractors to acquire ownership rights to the software for existing unmanned systems and/or redesign the software architecture to decouple it from the platform and to implement an open software system that will increase flexibility for new missions and technology insertion over the system life.

Requirements and Development Recommendations. Based on its review, the Task Force makes the following recommendations:

- Military Services and the JROC should improve the requirements process to develop a mission capability pull for autonomous systems.
  - Explicitly feedback operational experience with current unmanned/autonomous systems to develop future requirements.
  - Use the autonomy reference framework to assess system concepts/designs at program approval.
- USD(AT&L) should ensure that future unmanned systems development programs are structured to capture the benefits of autonomy.
  - Establish programs to develop autonomous systems capabilities separately from the acquisition of the platforms they control. Acquire full government ownership and required documentation using open software techniques so that the autonomy capability can be maintained, upgraded to insert new technology and evolved to support new missions by any contractor, laboratory or government agency without being constrained to working with the original developer.
  - Support and accelerate DoD and Service efforts to develop common, open software operator control systems capable of managing multiple different platforms.
  - Direct that system designs explicitly address human-system interaction and delegation of decisions within the mission context.
- Each Military Service should initiate at least one open software design project, preferably for an existing platform, that decouples autonomy from the platform and deploys proven technology to reduce manpower, increase capability and adapt to future missions.

4.2. Test and Evaluation

Autonomous systems present significant, unique challenges to the DoD test and evaluation community. As the level of autonomy increases, test and evaluation needs to transition away from the execution of specifically planned scenarios to a new test paradigm that must be established to understand and validate the decisions made in a dynamic environment. The challenges facing the T&E community include the ability to evaluate emerging autonomous systems' safety, suitability and performance, as well as human interaction with autonomous systems. The T&E community must be able to predict a systems behavior and decision processing. The community must also be able to characterize the environment in which the autonomous system will operate and evaluate the ability of those systems that are sensing the environment and formulating a world model based on this sensed environment. The test technology community must advance the technology readiness levels of key supporting technologies and processes needed to improve DoD's T&E capability.

Traditional test programs have been focused on repeatedly performing a test, measuring a response and comparing that response to a documented performance specification. Testing perspectives need to shift to a perspective that is more broadly mission based and assesses the ability of the autonomous system to meet mission goals. The framework employed for testing must provide leeway to the system to adapt plans to achieve mission goals in a variety of ways that cannot necessarily be predetermined. The fact that the system's software reacts to external stimuli and makes non-scripted, but bounded, decisions is particularly challenging to the test community that is used to executing testing in a fully scripted sense. The ability of the T&E community to react to this changing paradigm is limited by the understanding of how autonomous systems truly make decisions. The DoD T&E workforce must be enhanced with new skills for robotics, artificial intelligence, networking and systems engineering for autonomous systems.

To meet the challenges for evaluating the performance of autonomous systems, a much broader understanding of the systems decision making capability is needed. A systems engineering approach is needed to plan and analyze autonomous system tests. The reference framework provides the foundation for this approach. Test and evaluation personnel must be able to predict the decisions that may be made by the autonomous system and gather enough data during the execution of test scenarios to validate the decisions made by the system. This is particularly critical in the evaluation of systems operating in a collaborative environment in which the decisions made by one system may be impacted by the decisions made by another autonomous system.

The T&E community must improve its test planning capabilities and processes for autonomous systems. It is critical to develop and integrate predictive models of autonomous system behavior that can easily be adapted to a specific system under test. This modeling will enhance the fundamental understanding of potential system reactions to the external environment and can include the systems reactions to subsystem failures. The test planning process must be enhanced to develop more rapidly detailed autonomous system test plans and enhance safety for autonomous system testing. The ability to predict autonomous system behavior will not be absolute. The prediction will always include some level of uncertainty due to the nature of autonomous systems' reactions to the external environment. The models must characterize the uncertainty included in any prediction. The simplest example is IBM's Watson system that competed on the game show 'Jeopardy!' Watson provided its best estimate of the answer to a given question and also presented the basis for its decision and the confidence level of that decision. The predictive modeling employed for test planning and execution must present the test execution and analysis team with the same type of information to allow the team to make the best execution decisions possible.

The role of autonomous systems is changing from a tool to a fully functional teammate in execution of a tactical mission. As a result, autonomous systems will be interacting with their human teammates at an increasing pace. Test technologies must be developed that enable an understanding of this interaction. The autonomous systems will not solely be providing information for decisions to humans but will be able to exchange information of its understanding of a situation as well as accept information from a human teammate to aid or influence its decisions. Current technology is limited in the measurement and understanding of the exchange of information between human and autonomous system teammates and the degree to which that information impacts decision making. It is also critical to understand the impacts of reduced or delayed communications between teammates on these decision processes. The ability to assess the cognitive workload and efficiency of the manned-unmanned teams is critical in operational testing.

Open-air testing of autonomous systems is greatly limited by the safety practices currently used on DoD test ranges. For unmanned systems to date, the DoD test range safety typically uses methods for containment of the system under test (SUT) to specifically defined operational areas. These operational areas are determined by the scripted flight (and ground) paths established during the planning process. Deviation from these scripted paths often results in the test being aborted and, in many cases, the SUT being destroyed or damaged due to the activation of termination systems. Test ranges have had some success in implementing a risk-based safety system, mostly in the area of long range missiles. Risk-based safety provides the methodologies for evaluating risk to the general public, range workers or high value equipment and facilities based on a thorough understanding of the system dynamics and potential failure modes. This methodology has increased the flexibility of test ranges to execute larger scale operations. However, the inability to effectively model the behavior of autonomous systems with sufficient fidelity greatly limits the application of risk-based safety methodologies for autonomous capabilities.

Advancements are needed in test range instrumentation. The ability to instrument a system, or collection of systems, is critical to obtaining the necessary data needed for a thorough evaluation. Technologies for embedded instrumentation and non-intrusive instrumentation must be advanced. New Time-Space-Position-Information (TSPI) systems are needed to collect critical data in all operational conditions (e.g. GPS-denial) where autonomous systems will be tested. Finally, new capabilities are needed to effectively validate the autonomous systems sensing of the environment.

Test and Evaluation Recommendations. The Task Force recommends that USD(AT&L) review the current test technology programs, including those of the Test Resource Management Center, to ensure that the unique test requirements of autonomous systems are addressed. Among the topics that should be considered are:

- Creating techniques for coping with the difficulty of defining test cases and expected results for systems that operate in complex environments and do not generate deterministic responses.
- Measuring trust that an autonomous system will interact with its human supervisor as intended.
- Developing approaches that make the basis of autonomous system decisions more apparent to its users.

■ Advancing technologies for creating and characterizing realistic operational test environments for autonomous systems.

■ Leveraging the benefits of robust simulation to create meaningful test environments.

Based on the results of this research, it is likely that the Department will need to improve its operational test ranges so that they can better support the evaluation of autonomous systems.

4.3. Transition to Operational Deployment

Because the demands of conflict in Iraq and Afghanistan forced the deployment of prototype and developmental capability, the Military Services were unprepared for unmanned, autonomous systems at many levels. Spare parts were often unavailable, and logistics support, maintenance and manning concepts were not in place. The connectivity and bandwidth required to handle the enormous volumes of data collected by unmanned platforms, as well as the capability to process and distribute this information to all who needed it, were not available. (Processing and exploitation of large volumes of ISR data is itself an application that will benefit from autonomy, both by moving some of the processing to the collection platform and by exploiting AI techniques to increase the processing throughput of analysts.) The CONOPS and associated training were immature, often leaving the troops unprepared and unable to appropriately use everything provided to them. Also, usage evolved through operational experimentation in unimagined ways, such as illustrated by the significant impact of enabling the projection of force through arming Predator UAVs.

None of this is surprising, or particularly unique to autonomy, since similar experience has been observed with other advanced and new systems that were rushed into the combat arena because of urgent and compelling need. New challenges arise with the implementation of the January 2012 national defense strategy, which requires weapons systems and combat forces to be ready, rapidly-deployable and expeditionary so that these systems and forces can project power on arrival.

The continued war on terrorist organizations and their leadership—now globally dispersed and aware of the American UAV capability as well as electronic techniques—will be more challenging. New methods of supporting potentially austere (in terms of manning and support) forward deployments into even the most remote of landscapes will require new thinking and development of new deployment structures and manning to lower costs and footprint.

Trust in the capabilities built into our latest UxVs will be key to lowering manning requirements and, therefore, forward manning footprints. Developing operational trust between the users and the autonomous systems will require education and comprehensive training of the human-autonomy teams. This need is no different from the training of other crews, except that correcting deficiencies in autonomous system performance may require software modifications rather than changing tactics and techniques. When operational training of human-autonomous system teams begins, it is likely that new top-level requirements or changes to the CONOPS will be identified that will improve future teams. For example, the results of this testing may lead to a set of behavioral norms that improve human-autonomous system mutual understanding.

With proper planning and the appropriate tools, both development testing and operational training can begin well in advance of the availability of autonomous systems through the use of a surrogate machine system operated by a human. This will allow operators to refine concepts for employment and define their preferences in interaction, autonomy and physical capabilities of the machine system. Robust modeling and simulation tools are important enablers of this recommended early training. To date, primarily due to the needs of the current conflict, most operational experience has been with air and ground systems. This experience should also be relevant to the maritime and space domains.

For example, development of fully automated and autonomous capabilities to perform common functions like take-off, landing, navigation to target areas, avoidance of known threats (including the topology) and the ability to monitor a system's health and performance should be a given for a UAV that is not considered to be perishable. Operational trust is key to eliminating manpower to perform these same functions wholly or as a backup. As an example, use of self-formed and programmed alerts into the UAV can reduce or eliminate not only the manning for system monitoring, but also the requirement for linking system performance, maintenance status and other data back to operational centers. There is great potential for efficiency to be gained through such systems, which would eliminate connectivity requirements in combat theaters in which communication links and bandwidth are always at a premium.

UAV operators must take the opportunity to look at operational and tactical organizations to integrate, where practical, both unmanned and manned systems to eliminate personnel and support structure as well as the combined overhead of single unaligned deployment structures. For example, the U.S. Navy is integrating its UAV Fire Scout with the helicopter detachment on its new Littoral Combat Ships (LCS). The LCS provides the forward, remote basing of both vehicles, but supplements the helicopter detachment with some additional personnel to support the unique maintenance and operational requirements of the UAV. This teaming also allows for common mission integration and conflict resolution inside the operational missions of the vessel, as well as the elimination of standalone UAV manning.

Finally, all unmanned air systems should have, to some extent, the capability to use a forward-deployed sustainment model without rotation of the UAV to bases in the United States unless unique phased maintenance requirements are needed. This would allow inventory of UAVs to be balanced between the requirement for forward operations and a stable training inventory (relatively small) in CONUS bases. Employment of these concepts could potentially improve asset availability for deployment while driving down CONUS structure and manning as well as the total requirement for UAVs.

In addition to the mission benefits of autonomy, there are operational functions in which increased use of autonomy technology can reduce manpower and increase safety. For example, logistical support of forces requires multiple personnel to support each front-line warfighter. The Army Logistics Innovation Agency (LIA) is already taking forward-looking steps to incorporate autonomous/unmanned systems into the logistics chain to improve safety and efficiency. Expanding those efforts across Military Services will yield more viewpoints and likely result in many new opportunities. The largest gains, however, may only come from shifting the perspectives on how logistics is viewed

The U.S. military has done an amazing job meeting challenges to bring unmanned aircraft systems to an operational level of incredibly high competence and mission effectiveness. The caution here is to be not so closely wedded to the recent, first generation deployment structures and models. We have compensated for the challenges of our UAVs with an extraordinary level of manning and sustainment investments, and we need to move forward to meet the next challenges in our national security landscape.

Operational Recommendations. The Task Force recommends the following actions to achieve operational improvements in the usage of autonomy:

- Include sections about autonomous operations and their value in professional military education.
- Include unmanned, autonomous system concepts (in all domains—air, ground, maritime and space) in war games and pre-deployment operational training.
- Ensure that lessons learned from using unmanned systems in the current conflict are broadly disseminated and are formally reviewed by the Military Services for training and operational improvements for current systems.
- Develop a unified (all Military Services and domains) feedback mechanism in which operators can input experiences and recommendations on autonomous system performance and behavior during both training and mission operations so that common experiences can influence autonomous system design and human-system collaboration.
- Develop operational training techniques that explicitly build trust in autonomous systems and validate projected manning efficiencies.
- Invest in modeling and simulation capabilities required to support early operation training to influence CONOPS development, mission planning, training and logistics support.

5.0 Capability Surprise in Autonomy Technology

The use of autonomous UxVs may be the next "knowable" capability surprise. The Task Force found little evidence of planning or wargaming to counter potential uses of autonomy and UxVs, despite a significant investment by China and other countries.

This chapter provides an overview of the global market in land, marine and aerial UxVs and offers four symmetric adversary scenarios. It also describes the value of UxVs for asymmetric adversaries. The chapter discusses external and self-imposed vulnerabilities, concluding with four specific recommendations and two cautionary notes.

5.1. Overview of Global Unmanned Systems

Armed forces in the United States and around the world have actively embraced unmanned systems. The advantages of these systems in terms of persistence, endurance and generally lower costs and deployment footprint have been highlighted in recent conflicts. As a result, the world has recently seen the ever-greater deployment of UAVs, unmanned ground vehicles, unmanned underwater vehicles and unmanned surface vehicles on the battlefield. Unmanned systems have become an established part of military operations and will play an increasing role in the modern military machine.

To put the unmanned systems world market in context, the unmanned aerial vehicle market is by far the largest segment; unmanned ground, surface and underwater markets are funded at significantly lower levels (Figure 5-1). However, this picture could change rapidly. The market dynamic for ground and maritime systems appears to be driven by some of the same "tipping point" considerations faced by UAV systems years ago: waning cultural resistance coupled with increasing system capability and cost-effectiveness.

Photo Removed Due to Copyright Restrictions

Figure 5-1 Total U.S. Unmanned Systems Market by Platform

Should a significant triggering event occur, next-generation ground and maritime systems could emerge quickly on the scene, just as air systems have over the past decade. The potential size of these markets could increase substantially should international militaries choose to accelerate adoption of unmanned systems as they replace and modernize their forces over the next 15 years.

The most significant market is the United States, resulting from the enormous growth of interest in UAVs by the U.S. military, tied primarily to continuing operations in Iraq and Afghanistan. The U.S. will account for about three-quarters of RDT&E spending on unmanned systems technology over the next decade and about two-thirds of procurement. These levels of expenditure represent higher shares of the market than for defense spending in general, in which the U.S. accounts for two-thirds of total worldwide defense RDT&E spending and two-fifths of procurement. The unmanned systems market will likely repeat historical patterns of high-tech arms procurement worldwide, with Europe representing the second largest market, followed in turn by the Asia-Pacific region. It is possible that the Asia-Pacific region may surpass European levels of unmanned systems spending and development, but several significant players in the region, in particular China, are not transparent about their plans.

Unmanned systems development efforts are ongoing in Europe, Asia-Pacific and the Middle East. More than 50 countries have purchased surveillance drones, and many have started in-country development programs. In general, all of these lag the intense development efforts in the United States, but the increasing worldwide focus on unmanned systems highlights how U.S. military success has changed global strategic thinking and spurred a race for unmanned aircraft.

Photo Removed Due to Copyright Restrictions

Figure 5-2 China's first unmanned system model (Sources: Aviation Week, Dave Fulghum, Bill Sweetman)

In a worrisome trend, China has ramped up research in recent years faster than any other country. It displayed its first unmanned system model at the Zhuhai air show five years ago, and now every major manufacturer for the Chinese military has a research center devoted to unmanned systems. The latest pictures and models of unmanned systems from China show a reconnaissance truck with a joined wing and tail that could considerably increase range and payload and produce better handling at high altitudes. Roughly the same size as the General

Photo Removed Due to Copyright Restrictions

Figure 5-3 The latest pictures and models of unmanned systems from China show a reconnaissance truck with a joined wing. (Sources: James Simpson, Japan Security Watch, June 23, 2011)

Atomics Avenger, and powered by a single turbofan engine, this new UAV is the most advanced Chinese design seen to date and is the largest joined wing aircraft known to have been built. Much of China's efforts remain secret, but the large number of unmanned systems displayed at recent exhibitions, and very recent revelations on development and operational efforts underscore not only China's determination to catch up in this sector, but also its desire to sell this technology abroad.

In terms of evaluating the importance and pace of critical technologies such as autonomy and assessing the overall competitive state of unmanned systems with respect to potential threats for the United States, it is useful to examine the development of unmanned systems in China, which has taken place very rapidly, and is not constrained by many of the normal political processes found in democratic governments in the United States and Europe.

Photo Removed Due to Copyright Restrictions

Figure 5-4 U.S. analysts suggest that the new Chinese UAV design — with its 60,000-ft. cruising altitude, 300-mi. radar surveillance range and low radar reflectivity (if it uses the right composite structure) — could serve as the targeting node for China's anti-ship ballistic missiles.
(Sources: Aviation Industry Corp. of China, Shenyang Aircraft, Defense News, Defence Professionals, People's Daily, Aviation Week. Alberto Cuadra and William Wan — The Washington Post. Published on July 4, 2011)

China has shown an interest in keeping abreast with international developments in military technology, and the use of UAVs by the United States in Afghanistan in 2001-02 and in Iraq in 2003 has no doubt been noticed. China has had an active UAV program since the mid-1990s. However, data on the actual extent of UAV production is nearly non-existent, and there is little available information on China's overall procurement objectives. Therefore, any assessment of Chinese acquisition of military UAVs is bound to be speculative given the lack of data on the programs.

Recently, while observing a Chinese naval fleet passing between Miyakojima and the main island of Okinawa during a recent training mission, a Japanese Maritime Self Defense Force (MSDF) aircraft spotted a UAV flying in the vicinity of the fleet and took photographs for further confirmation. The UAV is believed to have taken off and landed on the deck of one of the vessels. After many years of displaying unmanned systems

Figure 5-5 A Japanese Maritime Self Defense Force (MSDF) aircraft crewmember spotted a UAV flying in the vicinity of a Chinese naval fleet. The UAV is believed to have taken off and landed on the deck of one of the vessels.

models at international air shows, and recent evidence of prototype and operational systems, it is clear that China is moving rapidly to catch up—and perhaps ultimately overtake—the West in this rapidly growing and increasingly important sector of aerospace and defense. In this defense-dominated field, China cannot look (openly) to the West for technical expertise and experienced suppliers, as it has done in the commercial airliner sector, and therefore it is evident the Chinese are copying other successful designs to speed their development of unmanned systems and rapidly apply lessons learned.

The scope and speed of unmanned-aircraft development in China is a wakeup call that has both industrial and military implications. U.S. exports of unmanned systems are highly constrained. China, with no such constraints, has made UAVs a new focus of military exports. It is difficult to establish the extent to which China's unmanned systems are operational, and it appears today that China is technologically lagging behind U.S. and other international efforts. Nevertheless, the military significance of China's move into unmanned systems is alarming. The country has a great deal of technology, seemingly unlimited resources and clearly is leveraging all available information on Western unmanned systems development.   China might easily match or outpace U.S. spending on unmanned systems, rapidly close the technology gaps and become a formidable global competitor in unmanned systems.

5.2. Unmanned Symmetric Adversary Scenarios
Symmetric adversaries are foes of the U.S. who presumably have similar aims and objectives and would employ similar kinds of systems in any conflict. Four possible scenarios come to mind.

Direct Attack on CONUS. UxVs (unmanned "systems" comprising: UAVs, UGVs, UUVs and USVs), could be used against CONUS for the same reasons the United States might choose them in the reciprocal case—reduced friendly casualties; increased availability of systems in the battle area (lack of human physical limitations allows air-refuelable UAVs to stay airborne longer or fight from a greater stand-off range, thus enabling more average aircraft on station for a particular task over time at equal cost); increased instantaneous force size (assuming a cost advantage to the equivalent manned system), etc. Enablers for their use would be characteristics like stealth or threat jamming systems—the same as exist for U.S. systems. Defensive challenges to the U.S. would be to overcome whatever numerical advantage, if any, the UxVs afforded the adversary. U.S. forces would have to be sized to meet the threat. A conflict with high attrition rates would eventually favor the force with more UxVs if manned system training requirements exceeded the time needed to manufacture unmanned systems.

Basing would be the key limitation for a peer enemy. Unless the enemy successfully fields both carriers and a carrier-based UAV, he will likely be limited to either large/refuelable long-range systems, or to operating from some small number of known and observable local bases (e.g., Cuba). This factor alone is likely to limit attack effectiveness against CONUS.

Assuming the enemy could launch an attack, the United States is currently well positioned to deal with Predator/Reaper size UAVs from the standpoint of air defense. High altitude systems, such as the Global Hawk UAV, could pose a problem as the United States has not encountered a manned threat in that regime since the Soviet-era MIG-25 Foxbat. High altitude/stealthy vehicles would be a significant defensive challenge, but they are unlikely to be compatible with effective stealth through the relevant future.

Overall, we do not anticipate enemy UxV forces significantly changing the calculus for this scenario in the near or mid-term.

U.S. Attack on Adversary Homeland. The adversary has many UxV options to oppose a U.S. attack. As in the parallel CONUS case, basing is the largest issue for the U.S. It is generally accepted that land bases within moderate range of a peer adversary will likely be closed, or at least badly degraded, in the event of a conflict. In the Pacific, at least, this has motivated new initiatives in long-range carrier-based attack, relying on carrier mobility and location uncertainty to sustain survivability. Consequently, an adversary might well structure UxV forces to support targeting of our Carrier Strike Groups (CSGs). Given the range of aerial, surface and subsurface candidates—as well as dispensable sensors—available this would be a very serious threat, and it could also plausibly include non-trivial organic attack capability. This threat could be extended to rear echelon supply convoys and other combat support assets which have not had to deal with an airborne threat in generations. Higher levels of on-board autonomy would circumvent our abilities to degrade UxV performance by simply jamming the adversary C2 links.

With respect to actual defense of the adversary's homeland, the adversary's choice of UxVs would more likely be based on its ability to generate (and sustain) a larger instantaneous force size at lower cost (assuming adequate tactical performance) to make the U.S. attack as expensive and difficult as possible. Reduced training costs would be particularly significant both in maintaining an adequate defensive posture over time and in response to high attrition. In any longer-running campaign, human losses and exhaustion will eventually become an issue. UxVs can substantially contribute to multiple points on the defensive kill chain, without regard to human losses or fatigue. The mere existence of a large UxV force element in a peer's integrated defense system would substantially complicate U.S. mission planning and execution. Unmanned platforms lost to attrition might also be easier to replace than manned platforms. Close in basing would remove any enemy dependency on satellite communications, thus removing a significant degree of vulnerability.

Regional Warfare (i.e., attacks on U.S. forces outside the CONUS). The scenario considers one similar to that faced by the United States during the Korean War, in which U.S. and a symmetric adversary or an adversary client's forces were fighting on third-party territory, and the adversary homeland was a sanctuary. The adversary would likely see the value of UxVs in a similar manner to its view of UxVs' utility in attacking the CONUS—fewer casualties, larger instantaneous and average-available forces in the theater and opportunities to find and engage U.S. naval forces. In this case, however, the adversary would expect to have sufficient basing, as well as home sanctuaries from which to sustain its UxV fleets. The training cost argument could be less compelling if, as might be expected, the number of forces deployed in such a conflict was small compared to the total available in garrison. If the distance from adversary homeland were short, UxVs could be operated from sanctuary directly into the battle space. This would enable application of large numbers of small systems, conferring significant advantage if they were capable of surveillance, attack and/or electronic/cyber warfare. Defending against large systems would pose the same challenges as in the case of an attack on CONUS. Defending against a proliferation of small systems while operating our own manned and unmanned systems would be complex and represent a serious threat.

Actions Short of Active Warfare to Gain Military Advantage in Case of Hostilities. In this scenario the value of UxVs to the adversary would be to extend, supplement or replace the capabilities of overhead systems to provide extended range detection and tracking of U.S. forces. UxVs for these purposes would not have to be stealthy and would not need strike or defensive capabilities so the cost would be much less than manned systems for equal coverage. Broad Area Maritime Surveillance (BAMS)-like systems for tracking U.S. ship movements would be an effective way for a near-peer to force carrier battle groups to stand off significant distances. They could also track troop buildups and harass supply lines. The combination of space-based queuing assets with long-range, long-endurance surveillance UxVs could add substantially to U.S. attack vulnerability at the outset of conflict.

5.3. Value for Asymmetric Adversaries

The UxV value to our asymmetric adversaries is arguably more dramatic than for any near peers. All of our efforts to reduce integration time and barriers to entry for U.S. defense suppliers of unmanned systems also allow less sophisticated enemies into the game. A crude analogy for this is the process by which the internet removed the barriers for command and control (C2) and ISR. Inexpensive but increasingly capable small systems allow new opportunities for adversaries to attack U.S. forces and interests around the world. Inexpensive and easily manufactured systems also provide tactical and strategic persistence to adversaries who can now easily make and deploy such systems as fast as the United States can interdict and destroy them without the equivalent cost burden of defensive systems.

On the battlefield, the use of small UxVs, particularly in large numbers, could create significant harassment and confusion even if only a few had actual ISR, strike, chemical or biological weapons or electronic warfare/cyber war capability. For UAVs, the U.S. currently has limited dedicated defensive capabilities other than fighters or surface-to-air missiles (including MANPADS), giving the enemy a significant asymmetric cost advantage. Surface and underwater defense would rely on similarly asymmetric exchange ratio options by emphasizing the use of small UxVs. The United States has soldiers with weapons and helicopter gunships that could be pressed into service, and the country has placed Stingers on Predators and fired them at air targets. There are many potential lower cost solutions that have not yet been fielded or included into U.S. systems (tactics, doctrine and training).

While the proliferation of small, capable UxVs presents an asymmetric defensive challenge, the biggest operational problem may be that large numbers of enemy UAVs would complicate control and management of our own offensive air assets. Today's systems fly blind with respect to other UxVs in their vicinity. Just flooding the airspace with simple UAVs flying random patterns would create the equivalent of a flock of geese at the end of a commercial runway.

Development of any effective, real-time enemy unmanned ISR capability—even at the local level—would severely erode the ISR advantage essential to the U.S. tactical maneuver scheme. It would make it more difficult to force contact on U.S. terms, and it could expose U.S. forces to surprise attack or ambush. To the extent that enemy UAVs presented a credible strike capability and, absent air supremacy, U.S. forces could be forced to disperse and rely on unit-level air defense. This would limit mobility, the ability to effectively concentrate forces and dilute offensive firepower. Even if the capability were not widespread, the tactical advantage could potentially shift to the enemy at least in locales.

In CONUS, as Peter Singer points out in "Wired for War," asymmetric foes could smuggle in or build cheap UAVs and program them to fly over military or other sensitive installations either for lethal effects or just harassment. This would probably not provide much actual military counterforce utility, but the popular alarm and resulting political effects could rival that of 9/11. If the asymmetric adversary definition is extended to include drug cartels and other forms of organized crime, the potential for "misuse" expands rapidly.

These kinds of adversaries also benefit from lower institutional barriers to using new technologies. Issues such as safety and surety are likely to be less important, thus in principle these adversaries could selectively field advanced capabilities ahead of the United States.

5.4. External Vulnerabilities

In this section we consider external UxV vulnerabilities; namely, those that are imposed or can be exploited by U.S. enemies.

Dynamic threat and tactical environments demand the ability to quickly detect and assess significant events (includes own ship internal malfunctions as well as re-tasking/re-targeting or threat activity) and replan the mission as required to ensure survival and mission objective accomplishment. Remotely operated UxVs, with limited automated decision aiding in the ground station, are particularly vulnerable to slow mission re-planning timelines, exacerbated by C2 communication latencies or interruptions. The availability of autonomous on-board dynamic mission management (event detection, situation assessment and re-planning) capabilities for threat avoidance, contingency management, etc., would mitigate dynamic response issues as well as ensure appropriate response in the event of communications failures. In the meantime, less autonomous UAVs remain extremely vulnerable to dependence on satellite and/or line of site C2 links.

An extension of this satellite dependency is the ability to commercially attack the linkage. More specifically, a purely commercial act like outbidding the United States for the available commercial ultra-high frequency (UHF) transponders could result in enemy shut down of U.S. UxV capabilities.

Another, serious emerging vulnerability is from all forms of cyber attacks—from denial of service to taking over C2 of the actual platforms. At best, current UxV requirements deal with traditional information assurance aspects and not defense against offensive cyber attacks. This threat is compounded by the affordability pressures to use commercial off-the-shelf (COTS) and open source products in ground stations, and the increasing desire to network platforms and ground station locations. The dependence on commercial information technology hardware (processors, etc.) also exposes the UxV to the cyber vulnerabilities of the global supply chain.

The ability to inexpensively deny GPS to ground and low-flying air systems is a well known threat and will not be discussed here.

5.5. Self-Imposed Vulnerabilities

In addition to technical limitations and vulnerabilities, UxVs are operationally hampered by doctrinal and cultural issues. For example, UxVs frequently operate within the mind set of manned CONOPS, which are based on human physical and cognitive capabilities. Consequently, the United States might easily fail to exploit the full advantage of UxVs' unique capabilities. Among these self-imposed vulnerabilities are:

- Overly restrictive rules of engagement in general and legal issues for lethal use of unmanned strike.

- Lack of senior service champions (probably because they lack experience and familiarity with the potential capabilities of advanced systems and thus see excessive risk).
- High barriers to entry for small third party autonomy service providers.
- Architectural limits to simple update of existing systems. For example, the United States does not currently have systems in which component pieces can be inserted or replaced at will without requiring a re-design of the entire system.

The failure to:

- Consider novel approaches enabled by UxVs.
- Proactively address the cyber threat.
- Develop and train for defensive UxV operations—how to defend against enemy use of highly autonomous systems.
- Aggressively move advanced capabilities onto the platform (mostly because of concerns over maturity, robustness and effectiveness).
- Pursue technologies (e.g. information fusion for nuanced situational awareness, automated decision-making noisy or sparse information environments) which are particularly important to UxVs, but not to traditional/manned systems.
- Collect intelligence data on potential adversaries' unmanned systems capabilities.
- Conduct a robust experimentation program – wring out advanced capabilities in realistic experiments (red flags, national training center, etc), limited availability/use of manned surrogates to test and train with advanced autonomous features, refine tactics, evaluate threats, and then create another set of self imposed vulnerabilities.
- Finally, the DoD has dramatically reduced UxV funding after every major conflict since World War II. When the battle is won, budgets swing back to manned systems. A repeat of that historical pattern as the United States withdraws from Iraq and Afghanistan could be the biggest vulnerability of them all.

5.6. Recommendations

Despite the likelihood of this threat, the Task Force found little evidence of planning to counter adversary use of autonomy and unmanned systems against the United States. Unless this situation is addressed, adversary use of autonomous systems may be the next "knowable" capability surprise. Consequently, **the Task Force recommends:**

- DIA and the Intelligence Community develop threat assessments for potential adversaries that determine their posture and potential intent relative to the use of autonomous systems.
- The Military Services develop tactics, techniques and procedures for countering adversary use of unmanned capabilities. Specifically, include adversary use of autonomous systems in war games, simulations and exercises. This usage should not be constrained U.S. systems or rules of engagement

■ The Services also establish red teams to study U.S. systems and develop adversary responses.

In addition to explicitly preparing for adversary use of autonomous systems, greater attention should be directed to the vulnerabilities of the unmanned systems that are currently in the U.S. inventory or under development. All experience to date has been in benign threat environments with unchallenged air superiority. Specific vulnerabilities that development program managers and operators should consider are physical threats to the platform, jamming and cyber-attacks.

One final recommendation is in the form of a caution. There is a danger of "mirroring" here. The best counter to an advanced autonomous enemy UxV might not be a more advanced US UxV. As the United States continues to evolve its autonomous capabilities, it needs to remain open to the opportunities to employ them in unique and novel ways.

Appendix A—Details of Operational Benefits by Domain

A.1. Aerial Systems Strategy

The Strategy for the future Intelligence, Surveillance and Reconnaissance (ISR) enterprise of the United States has a single, ambitious goal: to achieve information dominance across the spectrum of conflict through cross-domain integration of ISR from air, land and maritime operations. Wide area sensors carried on airborne unmanned systems to include Full Motion Video (FMV), Signals Intelligence (SIGINT) and Ground Moving Target Indicators (GMTIs) have created an unprecedented amount of "big" data and integration challenges that can be addressed by the application of autonomous technologies. Likewise, the current unmanned Ground Control Stations (GCSs) and the distributed Common Ground Stations (DCGSs) have segregated displays and manpower-intensive analog functions that lend themselves to autonomy technology insertions. Manned and unmanned system joint operations are beginning to mature, and autonomy can help accelerate the synergistic benefit of these operations from dissimilar platforms. The current "autonomous technology focus" is too dispersed and uncoordinated within DoD to capitalize on proven autonomous technologies and aerial unmanned system concepts that will provide the United States an asymmetric advantage vital to the execution of its national security interests.

Vision: Unmanned aircraft systems have long held great promise for military operations, but technology has only recently matured enough to exploit that potential. DoD's 2012 plan calls for purchasing more of the existing unmanned aircraft systems for current operations, improving the systems already in service and designing more capable unmanned aircraft systems for the future. No weapon system has had a more profound impact on the United States' ability to provide persistence on the battlefield than the UAVs. From a low of 54 deployed unmanned systems in 2001 to nearly 8,000 systems in 2011, this unprecedented growth can be attributed to a dual commitment by government and industry to ensure our deployed forces had unquestioned decision dominance on the battle space, as evidenced during the last 10 years of continuous combat operations. Most of the unmanned growth has been in Group 1 and Group 2 unmanned systems. These smaller, less expensive unmanned systems have become an integral and essential tool for ground forces and have proliferated throughout the operational environment. Combatant Commanders continue to place high priority on deploying more unmanned systems in their respective Areas of Operations (U.S. Central, African and European Commands), and this Task Force does not see a diminishing of the need for additional unmanned systems.

The air domain has received the greatest concentration of visibility as DoD has embraced unmanned technologies. Table A-1 (below) shows that Unmanned Aerial Vehicle (UAV) investments will continue to consume a large share of the overall DoD investment in unmanned systems. Over the next 10 years, the Department of Defense plans to purchase 730 new medium size and large unmanned aircraft systems based on designs currently in operation, while improving the unmanned aircraft already in service. This investment represents an

DSB TASK FORCE REPORT DSB TASK FORCE REPORT
The Role of Autonomy in DoD Systems
Appendix A—Details of Operational Benefits by Domain| 78

inventory increase of 35%; today the Department of Defense has more than 8,000 unmanned systems. The Congressional Budget Office has estimated that completing the unmanned systems investments for which there are detailed plans will required approximately $36.9 billion through 2020. Worldwide, more than sixty countries are manufacturing unmanned systems. Fifty countries are designing unmanned systems and there are over 600 different models of unmanned systems worldwide.

Table A-1 2011 President's Budget for Unmanned Air Systems ($Mil)

		Unmanned Funding ($ Mil)					
Fiscal Year Defense Program		FY11	FY12	FY13	FY14	FY15	Total
Air	RDTE	1,106.72	1,255.29	1,539.58	1,440.57	1,296.25	6,638.40
	PROC	3,351.90	2,936.93	3,040.41	3,362.95	3,389.03	16,081.21
	OM	1,596.74	1,631.38	1,469.49	1,577.65	1,825.45	8,100.71
Domain Total		6,055.36	5,823.59	6,049.48	6,381.17	6,510.72	30,820.32

These investment decisions have resulted in the fielding of a large number of unmanned systems capable of executing a wide range of missions. Originally, UAV missions focused primarily on tactical reconnaissance; however, this scope has been expanded to include most of the capabilities within the ISR and battle space awareness mission areas. UAVs are also playing a greater role in strike missions, as the military departments field multiple strike-mission-capable weapon systems for time-critical and high-value targeting.

Current Operations: Most unmanned system units are operating twenty four hours a day/365 days per year. Operators and sensor operators are maintaining a surge tempo and have curtailed training to provide the requisite combat air patrols required by current operations. Unmanned mission planners have embraced a "sense, sight and strike" operational concept. Once an unmanned system sensor operator identifies a high-value target, the Combined Air Operations (CAOC) J-5 makes the kill determination in accord with the Combatant Commander's priorities. Once a kill chain nomination has been initiated, the unmanned system operators are agnostic on which platform delivers the ordinance—as long as it is timely. Since most unmanned systems have enhanced loiter times, it is always preferable to have other assets make the initial kill and save the onboard unmanned system Hellfire missiles, GBU-12s and GBU-38s until absolutely needed. Operational concepts and tactics continue to evolve by theater, and each unmanned crew must be conversant with up to three Rules of Engagement (ROEs) and Special Instructions (SPINs) procedures. Recent operations have included Iraq, Afghanistan, Libya and Somalia/Yemen. The Air Force operates some 57 unmanned system CAPs (a CAP is an orbit of 24 hours anywhere in the world). The Air Force has an objective to increase to 65 CAPs by 2013. The 65-CAP threshold is not a firm requirement, but an objective. Missions and national commitment will determine exactly how many caps will eventually be required. Additionally, the Army and the Navy have robust unmanned system programs that will continue to grow and support global national security operations.

In addition to the military missions referenced above, the Department of Homeland Security continues to use an expanding fleet of unmanned systems to monitor our national borders and assist law enforcement officials and first responders. The Department of State is using unmanned systems to support operations in foreign countries that are experiencing contaminated environments, such as monitoring the Fushima Diachi reactor in Japan. Other Government Organizations (OGOs) are using aerial unmanned systems for classified missions. For the first time ever, unmanned systems were flown at the 2011 Paris Air Show. Our potential adversaries are flying unmanned systems over our open-water aircraft carriers and embracing low-observable technologies (e.g., Dark Sword unmanned system built by the Chinese). The stealthy RQ-170 was reportedly on the scene with the takedown of Osama Bin Laden on 1 May 2011.[53] Unmanned systems will provide situational awareness at the 2012 Olympics in London.

Status: Over the past two decades, unmanned systems have matured and significantly increased the capabilities and effectiveness that can be applied to any contingency, disaster response, or operation requiring persistence and engagements in contaminated, dangerous environments. Both the Army and Air Force unmanned system inventories have amassed over one million hours respectively. In fact, the Air Force fleet of unmanned systems has accumulated over 500,000 hours in 2010. The Army primarily prefers on-scene organic control of its unmanned systems, while the Air Force prefers remote split operations. The 432nd Wing at Creech Air Force Base is the hub of the Air Force's unmanned systems operation with eight squadrons operating unmanned systems in near real time up to 7,000 miles away using satellite connectivity for positive command and control. The Army center of unmanned systems expertise is Fort Rucker and Fort Huachuca. The Navy primarily focuses its unmanned system operations at Pax River Naval Air Station. A significant portion of the kinetic kill capability in the CENTCOM area of responsibility (AOR) is provided by armed unmanned systems. The historic growth of flight hours for unmanned systems is shown in Figure A-1 below.

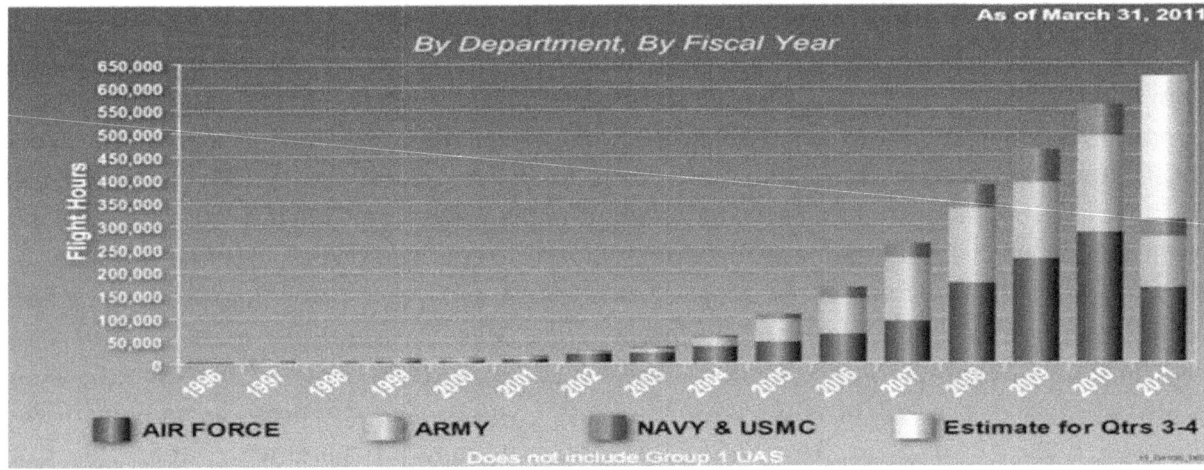

Figure A-1 DoD UAV Flight Hours

With the nominal 12-hour limitation of a human in the cockpit removed, the potential of unmanned systems to range great distances and maintain sensors and precision weapons over

---

[53] Lucey, Danielle. May 18, 2011. U.S. Officials Confirm Use of Sentinel in bin Laden Raid. AUVSI Magazine.

an area of interest for long periods of time represents a game-changing capability to provide situational awareness to all levels of command. Unmanned systems have blurred the distinction between operations and intelligence. Today, unmanned systems can simply out-wait an adversary or weather conditions and act accordingly when conditions permit. Along with unmanned systems' persistence capability, their relatively lower cost of operations provides a compelling argument to invest more and not less in these types of systems.

The DoD of FY2011-2036 Unmanned Systems Integrated Roadmap observes that warfighters continue to value the inherent features of unmanned systems, especially their persistence, versatility, and reduced risk to human life. The U.S. military services are fielding these systems in rapidly increasing numbers all domains: air, ground, and maritime. Unmanned systems provide diverse capabilities to the joint commander to conduct operations across the range of military operations: environmental sensing and battle space awareness: Chemical, Biological, Radiological, and Nuclear (CBRN) detection; Counter Improvised Explosive Device (C-IED) capabilities; port security; and precision targeting and precision strike. Furthermore, the capabilities provided by these unmanned systems continue to expand. The FY2011-2036 DoD Unmanned System Roadmap lists seven challenges for unmanned systems: 1) Interoperability, 2) Autonomy, 3) Airspace Integration, 4) Communications, 5) Training Standardization, 6) Propulsion and Power, and 7) Manned-Unmanned (MUM) Teaming. The Task Force has observed that today's iteration of unmanned systems involves a high degree of human interaction. It encourages DoD officials to pursue technologies and policies that introduce a higher degree of autonomy to reduce the manpower burden and reliance on full-time high-speed communications links while also reducing decision loop cycle time. The introduction of increased unmanned system autonomy must be mindful of affordability, operational utilities, technological developments, policy, public opinion, and their associated constraints. Likewise in 2010, the U.S. Air Force (USAF) released the results of a year-long study highlighting the need for increased autonomy in modern weapon systems, especially given the rapid introduction of unmanned systems. This study, "Technology Horizons," identified the need for greater system autonomy as the single greatest theme for future USAF Science and Technology Investment.

Findings: Unmanned aircraft clearly have a critical role in the future. Admittedly, the development of unmanned systems is still in the formative stage with more focus being given to sensors, weapons, and manned/unmanned operations than in the past. As DoD offices continue to develop and employ an increasingly sophisticated force of unmanned systems over the next 25 years, technologists, acquisition officials, and operational planners must prioritize their investments to focus on the greatest needs of the warfighter. A critical need cited by many of the presenters who briefed the Task Force was to promote integration of UAVs into the National Air Space. Due to Sense and Avoid technologies, redundant flight controls, experience, and revised procedures, the accident rate for most unmanned systems now mirrors manned aircraft. In addition, new missions for aerial unmanned systems are being seriously considered. The authors of the Reinventing Space Report from the Air Force Space and Missile Systems Center (SMC) cite unmanned systems as a reconstitution capability for the ever-increasing vulnerability of our space assets. Likewise, as other nations continue to develop and proliferate unmanned systems, there is a growing need for counter adversary unmanned systems weapon tactics. Key Task Force findings are:

- Autonomy can accelerate safe operations in the national air space
- Mission expansion is growing for all unmanned system groups
- Precision weapons are being added to almost all UAV medium and large unmanned aircraft systems
- There is a growing need for penetrating ISR systems to include the RQ-170 and others for operations in denied and contested environments Remote operations are placing increasing emphasis on satellite connectivity and bandwidth
- Big data has evolved as a major problem at the National Geospatial Intelligence Agency (NGA). Over 25 million minutes of full motion video are stored at NGA
- Unmanned systems are being used more and more in natural and manmade disasters
- Export control issues impact UAVs/autonomy/low observability and related technologies
- Homeland Security and other government agencies are increasing their investments in unmanned systems

Benefits: Unmanned systems will need to make use of their strengths and opportunities. As DoD continues to become more experienced in the employment of unmanned systems, operational concepts and tactics, and cultural and Service obstacles will become more manageable. The Department should be able to capitalize on system synergies and economies of scale. A better understanding of how best to employ the systems leads to a better understanding of the optimum mix of manned and unmanned systems as well as a better understanding of how best to employ them against a complex and changing threat environment. Key benefits include:

- Extend and complement human capabilities: The greatest operational attribute is endurance. The greatest programmatic attribute is affordability.
- Resilience: Unmanned systems offer incomparable resilience in terms of cross-decking sensors, replacement costs, and timely deployment.
- Reduced manpower: Creation of substantive autonomous systems/platforms will create resourcing and leadership benefits. The automation of the actual operation/fighting of platforms will decrease the need for people to crew them, while the personnel needed to simply maintain the vehicles is likely to increase.
- Reduce loss of life: The original concept for a fleet of unmanned systems was to have a mix of highly capable and moderately survivable systems as well as highly survivable and moderately capable systems. In high-threat environments, the need for manned aircraft will become diminished as sensor and weapons capabilities on unmanned systems increase.
- Hedge against vulnerabilities: Unmanned systems have an unprecedented advantage in persistence. Low-technology adversary missions such as cruise missile defense and countering of IEDs represent ideal growth missions for unmanned systems.

- Greater degree of freedom: The ability to function as either an ISR platform or strike platform in anti-access and denied areas represents a major breakthrough in mission flexibility and adaptability.

Current Limitations:

- Airspace Integration: Unmanned systems are not permitted to have unlimited access to our national airspace. The ability for UAVs to operate in airspace shared with civil manned aircraft will be critical for future peacetime training and operations.
- Reliability: The current commitment of combat forces has seen a number of unmanned systems fielded quickly without the establishment of the required reliability and maintainability infrastructure that normally would be established prior to and during the fielding of a system.
- Ground Control Stations: These stations are analog and do not make effective use of state-of-the-art autonomous technologies. Great opportunities exist in this area.
- Beyond-Line-of-Sight Communications and Encryption: There has been a significant increase in the amount of bandwidth required to support the expanding fleet of aerial unmanned systems. Likewise in this age of cyber warfare, new encryption devices are required.
- Onboard countermeasures: No aerial unmanned system carries any countermeasures. Incorporation of basic self-protection suites can maintain their survivability in anti-access and area of denial environments.
- Sensor exploitation: Today nineteen analysts are required per UAV orbit. With the advent of Gorgon Stare, ARGUS, and other Broad Area Sensors, up to 2,000 analysts will be required per orbit (see Figure A-2).

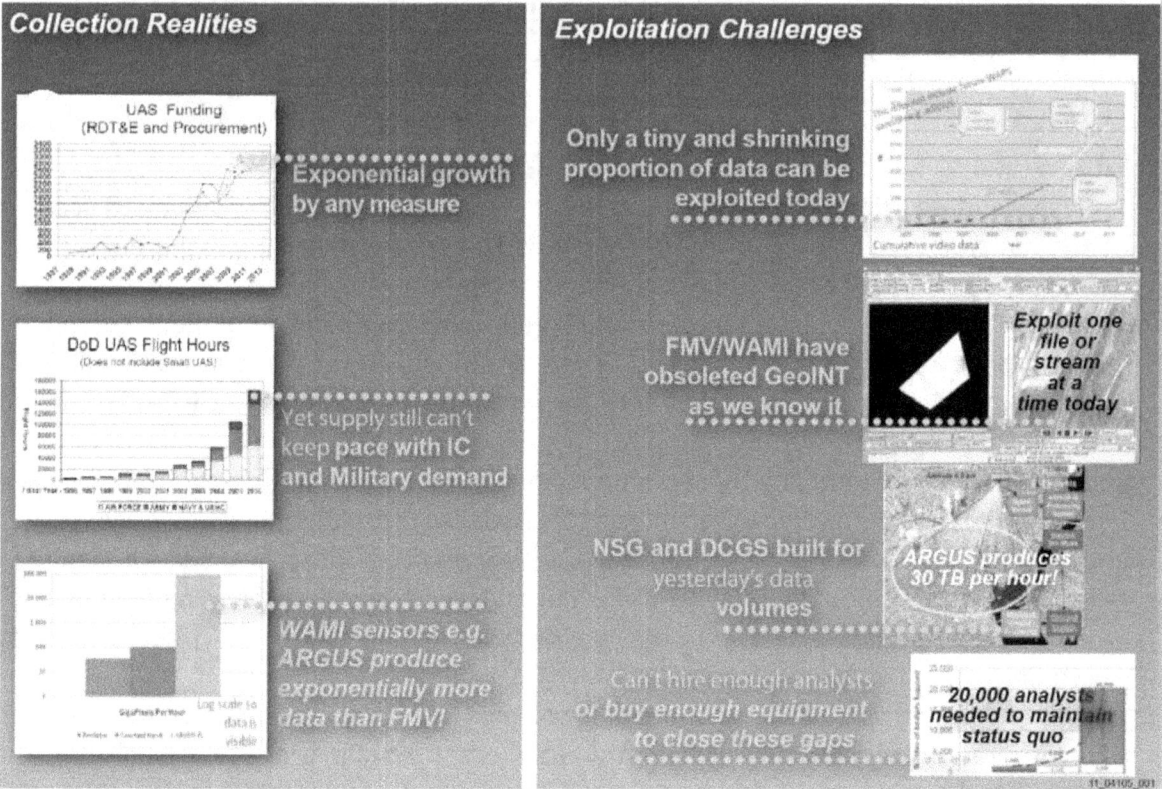

Figure A-2 Warfighter Current Limitations – Today's PED methodologies will not scale long term.

- More expedient integration into the national air space: A critical missed opportunity is allowing aerial unmanned systems access to U.S. National and ICAO airspace with roust onboard sense and avoid technologies.

- Trust of aerial unmanned systems: Unmanned systems are still a relatively new concept to most of the civilian population. As a result, there is a natural fear of a new and unproven technology with concerns about safety. This in turn creates difficulties for the Military Services to obtain approvals for proper test and evaluation of new systems or in some cases support for resourcing the acquisition of a new system.

- Command and Control: Integration of command and control of unmanned systems within existing and future battle command systems is not well understood.   The integration of the ISR products provided to battle command systems by unmanned systems and their distribution to the warfighters are not optimal.

- Training: There is no high-fidelity training environment for aerial unmanned system pilots and sensor operators. In fact, there is no computer-based training system for Predator crews that operate in conjunction with real-world weapons tactics training. A full simulation is not available and is sorely needed to ensure the level of proficiency of aerial unmanned crews is maintained. It takes the Air Force a full ten months to fully train a Predator crew member. The Army only requires three months. These vastly different approaches need to be reconciled and more focus given to using autonomy technologies to enhance training.

- Air Refueling: Global Hawk has developed an air refueling capability and this low-cost alternative to manned air refueling systems needs further evaluation.
- Potential air-to-air missions: As aerial unmanned systems evolve with the development and fielding of advanced systems such as the X-45 and X-47, air-to-air capabilities need to be considered and evaluated.
- Optionally piloted vehicle: This concept can significantly remove the limitations of operating over populated areas while reducing the cost (sustainment and loss of life) when operating in high-threat environments (adversary or highly contaminated).

A.2. Maritime Systems

Unmanned maritime systems can generally be categorized into two categories: unmanned surface vehicles (USV) and unmanned underwater vehicles (UUV). USV missions include antisubmarine warfare (ASW), maritime security, surface warfare, special operations forces support, electronic warfare, and maritime interdiction operations support[54]. UUV missions include ISR, mine countermeasures, ASW, inspection/identification, oceanography, communication/navigation network node, payload delivery, information operations, and time-critical strike[55]. The Navy's vision for USVs/UUVs is to seamlessly integrate them with manned systems in an effort to provide the fleet with both a cost-effective and competitive warfighting capability into the future.

The key to this vision is the development and fielding of unmanned surface and undersea maritime systems capable of long dwell missions. The Chief of Naval Operations (CNO) has a stated goal of 2020 IOC for UUVs to be capable of 30 to 70-day missions. In the near term, these systems will be brought into theater and commanded from host platforms (littoral combat ships (LCSs) and attack submarines (SSNs)). Eventually these systems will be capable of operating from forward deployed bases, transiting to their assigned area of regard, conducting operations far forward, and returning to port without the need for host platforms. They will augment and replace capabilities currently provided by surface combatants and submarines and free up those platforms for other tasks. This will extend/complement human performance by providing capability where humans are the limitation, e.g., persistent attention to task, better than human sensing, access to difficult/unacceptably risky locations, and rapid response.

Missions will initially evolve from short duration local operations in coastal areas, to medium duration open-ocean operations in constrained areas, to long duration operations in unconstrained areas. As capabilities mature, missions will transition to advanced covert operations, both collaborative and unassisted, and finally to advanced, weaponized operations, both covert and overt. Unmanned systems will be deployed across the detect-to-engage sequence, and will enable a shortened timeline to kinetic results. Unmanned maritime systems will be able to operate within the coastal waters of competitor nations and in close proximity to targets with a low probability of compromise. They will be serviced by the Global Information

---

[54] U.S. Navy. 2007. Unmanned Surface Vehicle Master Plan.
[55] U.S. Navy. 2004. Unmanned Undersea Vehicle (UUV) Master Plan.

Grid (GIG), and their relevant local operational picture both above and below the sea surface will be available to the command structure on a real-time basis. As a result, they will provide improved information and decision flow at the network edge.

In the far term, the development of an autonomous fleet consisting of coordinated packs of vehicles operating in concert with manned combatants is a distinct possibility. This class of unmanned maritime systems could provide a large fraction of the combat capability currently provided by manned assets, but in a reduced size, able to operate in a less risk-adverse posture and at a reduced cost.

Major S&T Investment: The Office of Naval Research (ONR) has kicked off as a GFY12 start, a four-year Innovative Naval Prototype (INP) program to address shortcomings in areas that are viewed as technological long poles to supporting long dwell missions (i.e., autonomy, endurance, reliability, and energy). In the autonomy area, the intent is to develop hardware and software that will allow large displacement UUVs to operate and survive in specified areas in the littorals for 70+ days without human interaction in the presence of all types of vessels and obstacles found in the littorals. Particular challenges include undersea obstacle avoidance; surface obstacle avoidance; automated characterization of surface vessel intent; fishnet detection, avoidance, and extraction; and the flexibility to address unexpected challenges that may arise during autonomous operations. The INP will conduct simulation and at-sea testing of the developed autonomy algorithms and sensors. At-sea testing will be done utilizing a full-scale government-operated UUV prototype.

The following table, from the Unmanned Systems Integrated Roadmap FY2011-2036 (published in GFY10), reflects the growing RDT&E and Procurement budgets to address the development of unmanned maritime systems over the FYDP.

Table A-2 President's 2011 Budget for Unmanned Maritime Systems ($ Mil)

Fiscal Year Defense Program		Unmanned Funding ($ Mil)					
		FY11	FY12	FY13	FY14	FY15	Total
Sea	RDTE	29.69	62.92	65.72	48.60	47.26	254.19
	PROC	11.93	45.45	84.85	108.35	114.33	365.90
	OM	5.79	4.71	3.76	4.00	4.03	22.28
Domain Total		47.41	113.08	154.32	160.94	165.62	641.37

Open-architecture, open-business models, common infrastructure: Also critical to achieving the Navy's unmanned maritime systems vision, is affordability over the breadth of missions and systems to be developed. To ensure cost-effective development, acquisition, and in-service support of future unmanned systems, the Navy is utilizing the Modular Open-Systems Approach (MOSA). MOSA is an integrated business and technical strategy that employs modular design and defines key interfaces using widely supported, consensus-based standards that are published and maintained by a recognized industry standards organization, and addresses interoperability, maintainability, extensibility, composability, and reusability. The overall open-architecture/business strategy includes acquiring appropriate contractual data rights from all developers; selecting common control software that is a Service-Oriented Architecture (SOA); requiring that all autonomy computer software configuration items (CSCIs) are SOA-compatible; and selecting an open, modular, vehicle-independent autonomy framework on which to base future advanced autonomy developments and a complementary common simulation infrastructure. This strategy mimics the highly successful and extremely cost-effective Advanced Rapid COTS Insertion/Advanced Processor Build (ARCI/APB) approach that has been developed and applied to submarine combat systems over the last decade and a half.

Current Status: The USV efforts of note are described briefly in Table A-3. In addition, there are many X-Class (three meters or less) USV developments, but all are remotely operated and therefore not detailed here. The following table, from the Unmanned Systems Integrated Roadmap FY2011-2036 (published in GFY10), captures the immature state of USV acquisition.

Table A-3 USV Capabilities by Program

System	Mission Capabilities	Acquisition Status
Autonomous Unmanned Surface Vehicle (AUSV)	Intelligence Surveillance and Reconnaisance/ Reconnaissance, Surveillance and Target Acquisition	Other
Mine Countermeasures (MCM) Unmanned Surface Vehicle USV	Mine Warfare/Organic Mine Countermeasures	Concept
Anti-Submarine Warfare (ASW) Unmanned Surface Vehicle (USV)	Anti-Submarine Warfare	Other
Sea Fox	Intelligence Surveillance and Reconnaisance/ Reconnaissance, Surveillance and Target Acquisition, Force Protection	Other
Remote Minehunting System (RMS), AN/WLD- 1(V)1	Mine Warfare/Organic Mine Countermeasures	Design & Development
Modular Unmanned Surface Craft Littoral	Intelligence Surveillance and Reconnaisance/Reconnaissance, Surveillance and Target Acquisition	Other

UUV efforts of note are described briefly in Table A-4 (systems currently in acquisition or operation, systems currently or soon to be available for experimentation, 21-inch diameter systems from prior programs of record (PORs), and commercially available systems). The following table, from the Unmanned Systems Integrated Roadmap FY2011-2036 (published in GFY10), captures the immature state of UUV acquisition.

Table A-4 Unmanned UUV Capabilities by Program

System (*Commercial developments)	Mission Capabilities	Acquisition Status
Sea Stalker	Intelligence, Surveillance & Reconnaissance/Reconnaissance, Surveillance & Target Acquisition	Other
Sea Maverick	Intelligence, Surveillance & Reconnaissance/Reconnaissance, Surveillance & Target Acquisition	Other
Echo Ranger*	Inspection & Identification, Oceanographic Survey	Other
Marlin*	Inspection & Identification, Oceanographic Survey	Other
Surface Countermeasure Unmanned Undersea Vehicle	Mine Warfare/Organic Mine Countermeasures, Inspection & Identification	Concept
MK18 Mod 2 Kingfish UUV System	Surface Warfare/Anti-Surface Warfare, Mine Warfare/Organic Mine Countermeasures, Inspection & Identification	Production
Surface Mine Countermeasure Unmanned Undersea Vehicle User Operational Evaluation System Increment 2	Mine Warfare/Organic Mine Countermeasures,	Other
Surface Mine Countermeasure Unmanned Undersea Vehicle User Operational Evaluation System Increment 1	Mine Warfare/Organic Mine Countermeasures,	Other
Battlespace Preparation Autonomous Underwater Vehicle (BPAUV)	Mine Warfare/Organic Mine Countermeasures,	Other
Hull Unmanned Underwater Vehicle Localization Systems (HULS)	Mine Warfare/Organic Mine Countermeasures, Explosive Ordinance Disposal, Inspection & Identification	Production
MK18 Mod 1 Swordfish UUV System	Mine Warfare/Organic Mine Countermeasures, Explosive Ordinance Disposal, Inspection & Identification	Sustainment
Large Displacement Unmanned Underwater Vehicle (LDUUV)	Anti-Submarine Warfare, Intelligence, Surveillance & Reconnaissance, Mine Countermeasures	Concept
MK18 Mod 1 Swordfish UUV System	Mine Warfare/Organic Mine Countermeasures, Explosive Ordinance Disposal, Inspection & Identification	Sustainment

Additionally the Sea Stalker program was initiated in FY08 to provide a system to be used for experimentation. It leveraged an existing 38-inch vehicle to demonstrate ISR capability from UUVs and was funded by the Navy Irregular Warfare Office (NIWO). A final demonstration was held in FY10 in conjunction with the USS Bainbridge (DDG-96). In FY09, the Sea Maverick program was initiated, leveraging an existing 48-inch vehicle to again demonstrate ISR capability from a UUV, as part of the Deputy Assistant Secretary of the Navy (DASN) command, control, communications, computers, intelligence (C4I) and Joint Interagency Task Force-South (JIATF-S) "Thunderstorm" project. A final demonstration was held in FY10.

A Defense Advanced Research Projects Agency (DARPA) project Collaborative Networked Autonomous Vehicles (CNAV) developed and demonstrated autonomous control methods for distributed platforms (UUVs) to execute various cooperative tasking in restrictive littoral waters.

ONR's Persistent Littoral Undersea Surveillance (PLUS) program has recently begun to transition and provides collaborative detection and cueing for ASW.

Other vehicles available for experimentation, in various states, include both the Near-Term Mine Reconnaissance system (NMRS) and the Long-Term Mine Reconnaissance system (LMRS) (each of these torpedo tube launch and recoverable products of prior PORs were defunded prior to OPTEVAL); Advanced Development UUV (ADUUV) (developed as the first phase of the Mission Reconfigurable UUV System (MRUUVS) POR); and the Battlespace Preparation AUV (BPAUV) (an ONR-developed 21-inch diameter platform that maps the ocean bottom near the shore, detects changes in in-shore conditions, and hunts mines).

Current Limitations:

- Autonomy: Current capability is adequate for either static/unstructured or dynamic/structured situations, but what is really needed is dynamic/unstructured capability. Today, what autonomy exists is usually tailored only for specific missions, users, and environments; has heavy reliance on preprogrammed plans and decision logic; and cannot be adapted easily to the unexpected or to broader missions. This contrasts with the goals of the ability to perform in uncontrolled environments with lower levels of supervision to accommodate the communications bandwidth limitation of the maritime, particularly undersea, environment; operate with uncertain information (imprecise, incomplete, contradictory, irrelevant); and operate in the open world where numbers and types of objects, agents, people are unrestricted, as well as unpredictable circumstances (may be non-cooperative or hostile with unpredictable adversarial behaviors).
- Perception/situational awareness is a key limiting factor: Autonomy algorithms are reasonably mature and capable, but the best planning and execution cannot overcome insufficient situational awareness. S&T needs to focus on sensor, signal processing, and exploitation development to fill this void.
- Lack of interoperability and commonality among manned and unmanned systems: There is a continual reinvention of capabilities by DoD programs, a significant gap

between the state-of-the-practice and the state-of-the-art, and a significant barrier to adoption by DoD and by defense contractors. With few exceptions, this has resulted in a failure to demonstrate the ability to reliably perform all aspects of extended duration UMV missions in concert with other manned and unmanned vehicles.

■ Vehicle: Lack of high-capacity, scalable, and safety-approved energy sources for long endurance missions: Without a 5-10x improvement in energy density over current state of the art, 70+ day missions are not feasible.

■ Insufficient communications: There is too little bandwidth and too many vulnerabilities to stress and disruption to take advantage of many ISR enhancements in sensors and exploitation.

■ Signatures and Anti-Tamper: Current platforms have little or no signature control and no provisions for anti-tamper.

Findings:

■ Many autonomy technology components have reached a sufficient level of maturity, but acquisition programs do not have distinct autonomy requirements: There is a firm belief in the community today that the majority of near-term missions can be accomplished without further autonomy development such that given specific mission requirements, it is entirely reasonable to expect that providers could today produce an 80 percent (or better) solution. In a related issue, the Navy Roadmaps for both UUVs and USVs are out of date (2004 and 2007, respectively), and do not reflect the CNO's vision for these systems.

■ Autonomy may benefit multiple program offices moderately rather than being a top priority of a single program office: Development programs are organized around stove-piped platforms or C4ISR systems rather than broader systems capabilities, the efficacy of autonomy development is low. Particularly with respect to autonomy, which is a software capability, there is a need to think in terms of mission capabilities instead of platforms or particular computer systems. The Navy's decision to combine the OPNAV Intelligence Directorate (N2) with the Communications Directorate (N6) into a single Information Dominance Directorate (N2N6) and to put all Navy ISR assets under their purview is an important step in addressing these concerns and should lead to a rationalized and cohesive set of requirements. The next step is to structure the programs to separate the acquisition of the autonomy software from the platform.

■ Autonomy is not a component or widget, it is a capability: The design and utility of a capability depends on the desired mission, the environment, manpower, costs, resiliency, and other "system-level" constraints (i.e., the ecology). Since autonomy is a capability that functions within an ecology, thinking of the software as a set of "plug and play" modules to be assembled on demand will likely introduce failures (both directly of the system and to distracting decision makers during the mission). Thus, there is a need for design principles or "meta" software to help match software functions to the ecology and explicitly states limits of operation.

■ Test and certification techniques that are appropriate for autonomous systems may be dramatically different from those used for manned platforms: The projected exponential growth in Software Lines of Code (SLOC) and the nondeterministic nature of many algorithms will lead to prohibitive costs to test exhaustively. In lieu of this brute force approach, timely and efficient certification (and recertification) of intelligent and autonomous control systems will require analytical tools that work with realistic assumptions, including approaches to bound uncertainty caused by learning/adaptation or other complex nonlinearities that may make behavior difficult to predict. Test and certification will need to prove not just safety, but also level of competence at mission tasks. This will require clearly defined metrics for stability, robustness, performance, controllability, for example), and the development of new tools for software verifiability and certification. Over time, machine learning will become an important aspect to autonomous system performance and will pose extreme challenges to test and certification of systems.

As a corollary to the above, there is a need for acceptance of nondeterministic performance and decision making by the test and evaluation community. Unmanned systems will operate in highly dynamic, unstructured environments, for which there are not computationally tractable approaches to comprehensively validate performance. Formal methods for finite-state systems based on abstraction and model-based checking do not extend to such systems, probabilistic or statistical tests do not provide the needed levels of assurance, and the set of possible inputs is far too large. Both run-time and quantum verification and validation (V&V) approaches may prove to be viable alternatives. Run-time approaches insert a monitor/checker and simpler verifiable backup controller in the loop to monitor system state during run time and check against acceptable limits, and then switch to a simpler backup controller (verifiable by traditional finite-state methods) if the state exceeds limits.

Most current systems have their own proprietary and/or unique software architectures/interfaces that make it very expensive to add new autonomy capabilities. There has been a lack of funding/prioritization for developing and enforcing common/modular/open-source approaches (though current initiatives are addressing this). Even when not proprietary, the government has generally not opted to buy the data/deliverables that would make it feasible for a third party to interface with that system without expensive support from the prime. The current and ongoing strategic emphasis on open-architecture, open-business models, and common infrastructure should address this over time.

Summary: Unmanned maritime systems are poised to make a big impact across naval operations. Though in its infancy, there is significant opportunity for this impact to grow. Autonomy's main benefits are to extend/complement human performance providing platforms to do the "dull, dirty, and dangerous" and the capacity to deal with growing volumes of ISR data and potentially reducing/aligning workforce. The requirements-driven development and transition of UUVs and USVs into the fleet can be expected to result in a more cost-efficient mix of manned and unmanned systems.

The major technical challenges for increased capability of unmanned maritime systems are perception, situational awareness, and bounded adaptability – maintaining the balance between brittleness and predictability. The vulnerability drivers are communication links, cyber, and lack of self defense. These areas must receive S&T investments if unmanned maritime systems are to meet their potential.

A.3. Ground Systems

Autonomous systems, defined broadly as Unmanned Ground Vehicle (UGV), which may include remotely controlled vehicles, have been used on the battlefield as early as 4000 B.C. by the Egyptians and Romans, in the form of military working dogs. Today, military working dogs are still employed on the battlefield (Figure A-3) as sensory prosthetics. Additional autonomous ground systems within the U.S. inventory include missiles, such as the Tube-launched, Optically-tracked, Wire command, (TOW) guided missile, introd uced in the later stages of the Vietnam Conflict and still in the current U.S. inventory. In all UGV, the system is designed as either a sensory-prosthetic weapon system or for gaining accessibility to areas inaccessible by humans.

Photo Removed Due to Copyright Restrictions

Figure A-3 Example of a biotic, UGV with enhanced mobility and sensory capability, a military working dog sniffing for explosives in a field fertilized with ammonium nitrate fertilizer.
Photo by Maiden Shah, Afghanistan 2009

Currently, the use of UGVs on the battlefield is not as commonly known as the use of UAVs. Further, UGVs in service have less autonomous capability than the range of UAVs primarily due to challenges in mobility, where the terrain of the battlefield is variable and more difficult to navigate than the air. Nonetheless, UGVs are desired by both the Army and Marine Corp to achieve:

- Risk mitigation;
- Accessibility to areas on the battlefield that are inaccessible by humans;
- Enhanced sensing capabilities coupled with unmanned mobility;
- A capability for the application of violence that is not humanly possible;
- Biotic/abiotic battle formations, where combat units are composed of both human war fighters and automation components.

In an era where children have increasing familiarity with digital technology, younger U.S. military personnel are comfortable with the user interfaces and have adapted well to the current use of unmanned systems. For example, in the Army, both UAVs and UGVs are currently operated by junior enlisted personnel. This observation has been shared by many within the unmanned systems community, both DoD and industry, and is illustrated by the proficiency displayed by U.S. troops in the Global War in Terror (GWOT), where an increasing number of unmanned systems have been fielded for the first time on the battlefield, where the fielding unit rapidly gains proficiency before deployment of the platform in a forward area. The ability of junior enlisted personnel in forward

Photo Removed Due to Copyright Restrictions

Figure A-4 A Foster-Miller robot is deployed to place a charge for a controlled detonation of an IED detected by a manned vehicle's sensor system. Note the standoff distance between the robot and the Mine Resistant, Ambush Protected (MRAP) vehicle. Tangi Valley Afghanistan, February 2009.

deployed locations to master new technologies in the form of UAVs and UGVs in a minimal amount of time highlights an advantage in adopting UxVs, in that the learning curve to their tactical deployment is reduced. This is illustrated by increased use of unmanned systems in ground combat, most notably in route clearance, counter-improvised explosive device (C-IED) operations. In many of these missions, the user has no familiarity with the system prior to deployment and user proficiency is gained during missions.

Robotics is currently filling some capability gaps on the battlefield. For example, C-IED and route clearance operations in both Afghanistan and Iraq have benefitted by several currently fielded systems, which range from robotic arms attached and operated from modified MRAP vehicles to remotely controlled robotic systems (Figure A-4).

A member of the Task Force completed a combat tour in 2009 for the Center for Army Lessons Learned, and conducted an extensive study of route clearance operations in Regional Command East. At the time, interviews with soldiers illustrated the importance of UGVs in route clearance operations, but also illustrated two

Figure A-5 EOD personnel in protective suit moves to inspect a culvert for an IED. Note the cement block dropped in front of the culvert as a barrier against robotic platforms.

important challenges with the current state of the technology. First, the primary issue noted by junior noncommissioned officers (NCOs) on route clearance teams was the inability to do field expedient modifications to the robotic systems. The NCOs suggested two reasons: 1) the platform may take it out of service during modification, or could accidently be damaged during modification and testing, rendering it inoperable, and 2) modifications were not authorized, and those soldiers 'signed' for the equipment, could be held financially liable. There were no field service teams in the area at the time; thus, the ingenuity of these soldiers was unrealized.

Second, the cost-ratio of countermeasures employed against robots used in counter-IED operations is not favorable. A common enemy tactic is to place IEDs in culverts underneath roads. Unsophisticated countermeasures, such as the obstacle illustrated in Figure A-5, often prevent robotic penetration. During ground operations, field expedient enemy countermeasures to our UGV may reduce the tactical advantage of such systems. Technical evolution of UGV platforms during a conflict may represent an asymmetric economic threat (compare the cost of the cement block in Figure A-5 versus the technological advance required to defeat it in a robotic system such as that depicted in Figure A-4).

Both of these points illustrate the need to develop UGVs that are amenable to cost-effective field-expedient adaptations at the hands of the user, or forward deployed service teams. It also suggests that doctrine regarding the use of UGVs may be required to evolve with the technology. The Task Force recognized that the functional drivers of filling capability gaps, interoperability between automated and manned platforms, and affordability constrain efforts to provide the warfighter with survivability, economy of force, and functional reliability. DoD's Unmanned Systems Integrated Roadmap[56] identified four key missions designed to meet the warfighter requirements and to focus developmental efforts to achieve the desired functional attributes of UGVs. These missions are 1) reconnaissance and surveillance, 2) target identification and designation, 3) counter-mine warfare, and 4) chemical, biological, radiological, nuclear or high-yield explosive (CBRNE) missions. While additional capability production documents (CPD) are being drafted for the use of UGV in urban scouting and breaching operations, close combat operations, facility security, casualty evacuation and logistical support, parallel efforts in these fields may not be cost effective.

UGVs in combat operations face two primary challenges: negotiating terrain and obstacles on the battlefield and, for autonomous systems, operating in kinetic operations within the Rules of Engagement (ROE). Terrain negotiation and obstacle avoidance falls into a category of mechanical capabilities coupled with pattern recognition, and problem solving skills in increasingly autonomous systems. Operations within an ROE, however, represent a higher order cognitive skill that must fall within the maneuver commander's intent. In the case of the latter, the development of autonomous systems with effective human-system collaboration to manage the delegation of these decisions, that may or may not change during the course of a mission or engagement, would appear to be an important milestone. While the engagement of a robot in a non-kinetic environment in the Third World may appear inappropriate, the development of autonomous ground combat systems to counter enemy ground combat systems is a realistic scenario which the Task Force recommends receive development priority.

---

[56] U.S. Department of Defense. 2009. FY2009-2034 Unmanned Systems Integrated Roadmap. Washington, DC: U.S. Department of Defense.

The Unmanned Systems Roadmap does not propose a strategy for, nor prioritize, technology development to counter adversary use of UGV technology, but with the observed fielding of UAVs by non-state actors in combat operations against, it is reasonable to assume that our battlefield opponents will soon field such technology. The Task Force feels strongly that development of counter-autonomy (CA) capabilities should be a high priority. Developing systems to counter adversary use of U.S. capabilities is a concept familiar to the Army's field artillery community, where counter-battery firing operations have been enabled by Q-36 radar systems and the more recent fielding of the Lightweight Counter Mortar Radar system.

The following table, from the Unmanned Systems Integrated Roadmap FY2011-2036 (published in GFY10), reflects the RDT&E and Procurement budgets to address the development of unmanned ground systems over the FYDP.

Table A-5 President's 2011 Budget for Unmanned Ground Systems ($ Mil)

Unmanned Funding ($ Mil)							
Fiscal Year Defense Program		FY11	FY12	FY13	FY14	FY15	Total
Ground	RDTE	0.00	0.00	0.00	0.00	0.00	0.00
	PROC	20.03	26.25	24.07	7.66	0.00	28.01
	OM	207.06	233.58	237.50	241.50	245.96	1,165.60
Domain Total		227.09	259.83	261.57	249.16	245.96	1,243.61

Summary: Abiotic unmanned systems may never replace a military working dog or the infantryman in counterinsurgency operations. The current Unmanned Systems Roadmap, at times, appears predicated on the assumption of battlefield dominance and heavily influenced by the state of the threats we face today in the GWOT. However, the Task Force recognizes that ground autonomous systems must be designed for the greatest threat on the battlefield; namely, that of a highly mobile, extremely lethal enemy autonomous system that lacks the higher-order cognitive capabilities to conduct combat engagements within the confines of international treaties and the Laws of Land Warfare. Thus, while there are important UGV capabilities that the U.S. can and should develop, we should not lose sight of the threat this technology poses if used by our adversaries and should develop countermeasures to the technology along with exploiting it for U.S. advantage.

A.4. Space Systems

The role of autonomy in space systems can be organized in two categories: types of autonomous operations (mission and satellite) and the specific cognitive functions allocated to the space systems. Mission Operations refer to the ability of a satellite and/or payload to execute assigned missions without operator involvement/intervention. Satellite Operations refer to the ability of a satellite (or satellite bus) to execute routine operations to keep the systems operating in support of the payload and mission (i.e., housekeeping). A system with a limited delegation of cognitive functions is unable to execute significant sets of functionalities/tasks without substantial operator involvement/intervention, whereas a system with delegation of more complex decisions to the autonomy software is able to execute a full set of functionalities/tasks without operator involvement/intervention.

However, instead of viewing autonomy as a delegation of decisions, the traditional view or measure of autonomy, particularly within DoD, has been restricted to predefined explicit behaviors and programs without an "understanding" of a situation or a desired outcome. While this restricted definition is adequate for operations in predictable environments, it breaks down in situations of increased uncertainty and non-determinism.

The current and future strategic environment of space is increasingly congested, contested and competitive. By way of example, "DoD tracks approximately 22,000 man-made objects in orbit, of which 1,100 are active satellites (see Figure A-6). There may be as many as hundreds of thousands of additional pieces of debris that are too small to track with current sensors[57]." These trends present significant challenges to predicting/planning operations for DoD platforms operating in space, and amplify the need for systems to be able to execute functionalities/tasks in an unpredictable, dynamic environment without operator involvement/intervention.

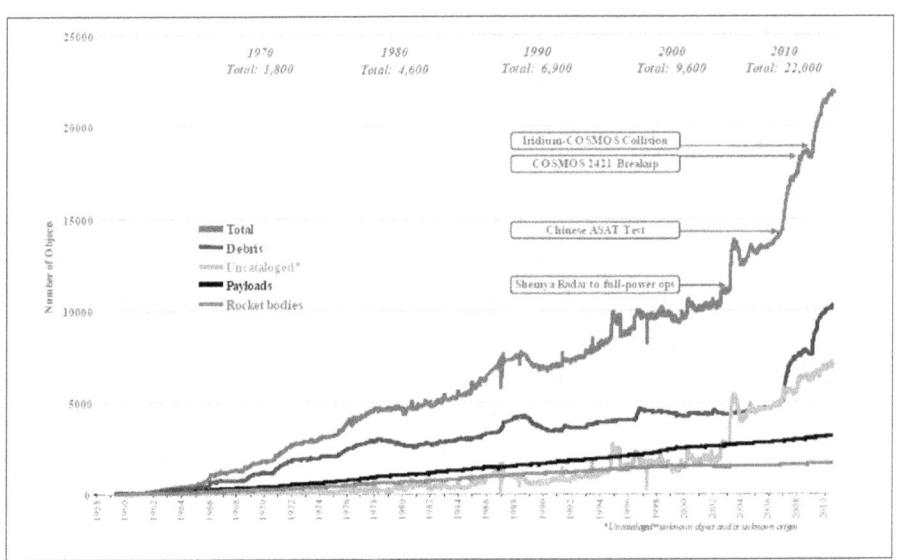

Figure A-6 Satellite Catalog Growth[58]

While space S&T efforts are undertaken by many government organizations, DoD and the intelligence community comprise the vast majority of organizations involved in space S&T, including the National Aeronautics and Space Administration (NASA), the National Oceanic and Atmospheric Administration (NOAA)and the Department of Energy (DOE).[59]

The Air Force Space Command, in particular, principally oversees the design, acquisition and operation of most DoD space systems. Currently, most, if not all, DoD space platforms operate

---

[57] National Security Space Strategy, January 2011
[58] National Security Space Strategy, January 2011
[59] GAO Study. January 2005. "New DoD Space Science and Technology Strategy Provides Basis for Optimizing Investments, but Future Versions Need to Be More Robust."

with only limited delegation of cognitive functions. Many capabilities reflect preplanned automatic responses, such as switching to backup systems, rebooting, scheduled downlinks and retransmission. Pre-planned, automatic responses are useful in that they can reduce manpower intensive processes, as well as enable systems to respond to foreseeable mission threatening events. They may even utilize expert systems and other advanced techniques to respond to those foreseen circumstances. However, preplanned responses can be very complex and can involve complicated decision-making, and they tend to break down when a system is presented with an unexpected circumstance. Consequently, Air Force Space Command has identified key future operational requirements for autonomy in space that are the basis for the development of future satellite systems, including:

- **Mission Operations:** Satellite performs significant portion of assigned mission without specific operator tasking, monitoring or intervention
- **Processing, Exploitation and Dissemination of Mission Data:** Data collected from space system processed, interpreted and disseminated with limited or no user intervention
- **Housekeeping:** Satellite performs basic housekeeping functions autonomously (e.g., battery conditioning, load shedding, eclipse operations)
- **Built in self-test, troubleshooting and repair:** Satellite detects, diagnoses and corrects problems automatically

Additionally, in 2010, the Chief Scientist of the Air Force published the Technology Horizons study, which identifies overarching capability themes, objectives and technological priorities that the Air Force must focus on over the next two decades to enable the Joint Force to be competitive in future operating environments.[60]

> *"The single greatest theme to emerge from "Technology Horizons" is the need, opportunity, and potential to dramatically advance technologies that can allow the Air Force to gain the capability increases, manpower efficiencies, and cost reductions available through far greater use of autonomous systems in essentially all aspects of Air Force operations. Increased use of autonomy -- not only in the number of systems and processes to which autonomous control and reasoning can be applied but especially in the degree of autonomy that is reflected in these --can provide the Air Force with potentially enormous increases in its capabilities, and if implemented correctly can do so in ways that enable manpower efficiencies and cost reductions."[61]*

Consistent with the operational requirements identified in the National Security Space Strategy, the Technology Horizons study underscores a number of technological challenges to overcome, including:[62]

---

[60] Technology Horizons, Volume 2; AF/ST-TR-10-02; 15 May 2010
[61] Technology Horizons, Volume 1; AF/ST-TR-10-01; 15 May 2010
[62] Technology Horizons, Volume 1; AF/ST-TR-10-01; 15 May 2010

- Developing robust, accurate, and comprehensive on-board automated planning systems capable of decomposing a high-level objective into a sequence of actionable tasks to achieve that objective; and designing rapid on-board satellite event analysis for real time reaction
- Designing techniques for semantic/contextual understanding of information; generating information and knowledge from integrated and fused data streams; and from this information set, determining the right information at the right time for the specific decision maker
- Integrating on-board satellite state-of-health monitoring, fault-detection and reasoning system to perform recovery from spacecraft abnormalities

Also among the findings of the Technology Horizons study is the point that achieving gains from use of autonomous systems will require developing new methods to establish "certifiable trust" in autonomy through verification and validation (V&V) of the near-infinite state systems that result from high levels of adaptability. The lack of suitable V&V methods today prevents all but relatively low levels of autonomy from being certified for use.[63]

The Task Force concurs that a new paradigm of validation is needed and envisions one that requires more field work and evolution/maturation, re-defining "certification." While developing trust is important, it may not require, or ultimately be in our interest, to formally prove systems will work a certain way to a near-infinite state. In fact, it is more likely the case that there are hidden assumptions in one's general approach that may prove to be the greatest source of problems, not the explicit stated coverage. There needs to be a balanced, risk-reward analysis in determining the extent to which a system's performance is proven. Moreover, S&T investments should emphasize continuous contact, continuous testing, and continuous evolution, rather than intermittent stops and starts. Continuous testing and effort in successive test-bed, is the kind of best practice that contributed to the success of DARPA's successful Grand Challenge program which aimed to create long-distance, driverless vehicles. DARPA's autonomous vehicle teams progressed from failing a somewhat simple desert task, to succeeding at a simple desert task, to performing on an urban task, to now the existence of a driverless vehicle. The key is to have a community pushing the bounds of interacting with the real world (in various levels), on a continuous basis.

Designing a satellite test-bed would be a good start toward achieving a continuous, successive and meaningful testing effort. Important to the successes of such an endeavor would be to reduce the barriers to entry for using the test-bed by making it understood to be a non operational effort.

---

[63] Technology Horizons, Volume 1; AF/ST-TR-10-01; 15 May 2010

Appendix B—Bibliography

Abbink, David A., Mark Mulder, and Erwin R. Boer. 2012. Haptic Shared Control: Smoothly Shifting Control Authority? *Cognition, Technology, and Work* 14: 19–28.

Adams, Julie A., Curtis M. Humphrey, Michael A. Goodrich, Joseph L. Cooper, Bryan S. Morse, Cameron Engh, and Nathan Rasmussen. 2009. Cognitive Task Analysis for Developing Unmanned Aerial Vehicle Wilderness Search Support. *Journal of Cognitive Engineering and Decision Making* 3 (1): 1-26.

Arkin, R.C. 2009. *Governing Lethal Behavior in Autonomous Robots*. Boca Raton, FL: Chapman and Hall/CRC Press.

Automatically Deployed Communication Relays (ADCR) Available from: http://www.public.navy.mil/spawar/Pacific/Robotics/Pages/ADCR.aspx

Autonomous Robotic Manipulation (ARM). 2012 Mar 29, 2012]; Available from: http://www.darpa.mil/Our_Work/DSO/Programs/Autonomous_Robotic_Manipulation_%28AR M%29.aspx

Bernard D, Doyle R, Riedel E., Rouquette N, Wyatt J, Lowry M & Nayak P (1 999). Autonomy and software technology on NASA's Deep Space One. 1999. Intelligent Systems. May/June: 10-1 5.

Billings, C.E. 1997. *Aviation Automation: the Search for a Human-Centered Approach*. Mahwah, NJ: Lawrence Erlbaum Associates Publishers.

Blum, A. and T. Mitchell. Proceedings of the 1998 Conference on Computational Learning Theory, July 1998; Combining Labeled and Unlabeled Data with Co-Training,"

Boularias, Abdeslam, Jens Kober, Jan Peters. 2011. Relative Entropy Inverse Reinforcement Learning. Proceedings of the 14th International Conference on Artificial Intelligence and Statistics

Bradshaw, J.M., C. Jonker, V. Dignum, and M. Sierhuis. 2012. Human- Agent Robot Teamwork (HART). *IEEE Intelligent Systems* 27 (1): 8-13.

Bradshaw, Jeffrey M., Paul J. Feltovich, and Matthew Johnson. 2011. Human-Agent Interaction. In *Handbook of Human-Machine Interaction*, edited by Guy A. Boy. 283-300. Burlington, VT: Ashgate.

Burke, J.L., et al. 2004. Final Report for the DARPA/NSF Interdisciplinary Study on Human-Robot Interaction. *IEEE Transactions on Systems, Man, and Cybernetics, Part C: Applications and Reviews* 34(2): 103-112.

Chandola, Varun, Arindam Banerjee, Vipin Kumar. 2009. Anomaly Detection: A Survey. ACM Computing Surveys.

Chapelle, O., B. Scholkopf, A. Zien. 2006. Semi-Supervised Learning. MIT press.

Christoffersen, K. and D.D. Woods. 2002. How to Make Automated Systems Team Players. In *Advances in Human Performance and Cognitive Engineering Research*, edited by E. Salas. Volume 2. 1-12. St. Louis, MO: Elsevier Science.

Chun, Andy, et al. 2005. Scheduling Engineering Works for the MTR Corporation in Hong Kong; American Association for Artificial Intelligence,

Adam Coates, Pieter Abbeel, and Andrew Y. Ng. 2008. Learning for control from multiple demonstrations. In Proceedings of the 25th international conference on Machine learning, pages 144{151.

Ghazizadeh, Mahtab, John D. Lee, Linda Ng Boyle. 2012. Extending the Technology Acceptance Model to assess automation. Cognition, Technology, and Work. 14: 39–49.

Darken, R. and B. Peterson. 2002. Spatial Orientation, Wayfinding, and Representation. In *Handbook of Virtual Environments: Design, Implementation and Applications*, edited by K. Stanney. 493-518. Mahwah, NJ: Lawrence Erlbaum Associates.

Davis, J.W., A. Morison, and D.D. Woods. 2007. An Adaptive Focus-of-Attention Model for Video Surveillance and Monitoring. *Machine Vision and Applications Journal* 18 (1): 41–64.

Department of Defense. 2009. FY2009–2034 Unmanned Systems Integrated Roadmap

Department of Defense. 2011. FY2011–2034 Unmanned Systems Integrated Roadmap

DSB Task Force on Improvements to Services Contracting, March 2011

DSB Task Force on Fulfillment of Urgent Operational Needs, July 2009

DSB Task Force on Creating a DoD Strategic Acquisition Platform, April 2009

DSB Task Force on Improvements to Services Contracting, March 2011

DSB Task Force on Department of Defense Policies and Procedures for the Acquisition of Information Technology, March 2009

DSB Task Force on Creating a DoD Strategic Acquisition Platform, April 2009; DSB Task Force on Fulfillment of Urgent Operational Needs, July 2009

S. Edelkamp, J. Hoffmann. 2003. Taming numbers and durations in the model checking integrated planning system. Journal of Artificial Research. 20: 195-238.

Ferris, T.K. and N.B. Sarter. 2008. Crossmodal Links Between Vision, Audition, and Touch in Complex Environments. *Human Factors* 5 (1): 17–26.

Gerevini, A., and Long, D. 2006. Plan constraints and preferences in PDDL3. In Proc. Int. Conference on Automated Planning and Scheduling (ICAPS- 2006) – International Planning Competition, 7–13

Gerkey, Brian P. and Maja J. Mataric. 2002. Sold!: Auction Methods for Multirobot Coordination. *IEEE Transactions on Robotics and Automation* 18 (5): 758-768.

Geyer, C.M., S. Singh, and L.J. Chamberlain. 2008. Avoiding Collisions Between Aircraft: State of the Art and Requirements for UAVs operating in Civilian Airspace. tech. report CMU-RI-TR-08-03.

Ghazizadeh, Mahtab, John D. Lee, and Linda Ng Boyle. 2012. Extending the Technology Acceptance Model to assess automation. *Cognition, Technology and Work* 14 (1): 39-49.

Goodrich, Michael A., Bryan S. Morse, Cameron Engh, Joseph L. Cooper, and Julie A. Adams. 2009. Towards Using UAVs in Wilderness Search and Rescue: Lessons from Field Trials. *Interaction Studies* 10 (3): 453-478.

Hawley, John K. and Anna L. Mares. 2012. Human Performance Challenges for the Future Force: Lessons from Patriot after the Second Gulf War.

Herz, Robert. 2010. Human Factors Issues in Combat Identification.

Hoffman, R. R. and D.D. Woods. 2011. Beyond Simon's Slice: Five Fundamental Trade-Offs that Bound the Performance of Human Macrocognitive Work Systems. *IEEE Intelligent Systems* 26 (6): 67-71.

Hollnagel, Erik, D.D. Woods, and Nancy Leveson ,eds. 2006. *Resilience Engineering: Concepts and Precepts*. Burlington, VT: Ashgate.

Hollnagel, Erik, J. Paries, D.D. Woods, and J. Wreathall, eds. 2011. *Resilience Engineering in Practice: A Guidebook*. Burlington, VT: Ashgate.

Hughes, T.C., et al. (in press). Multi-UAV Supervisory Control Interface Technology (MUSCIT): Spiral 3 Technical Report. AFRL-RH-WP-TP-2012-XXXX, Wright-Patterson AFB, OH.

Human Computation Workshop (HCOMP). in AAAI Annual Conference on Artificial Intelligence.

Intelligent Systems and their Applications. 1999. IEEE. 14(3): p. 10-15.

Johnson, M., J. Bradshaw, P. Feltovich, C. Jonker, B. van Riemsdijk, and M. Sierhuis. 2011. "The Fundamental Principle of Coactive Design: Interdependence Must Shape Autonomy." Coordination, Organizations, Institutions, and Norms in Agent Systems VI, M. De Vos, N. Fornara, J. Pitt, and G. Vouros, eds., Springer Berlin / Heidelberg, 172-191.

Johnson, M., J. Bradshaw, P. Feltovich, R.R. Hoffman, C. Jonker, B. van Riemsdijk, and M. Sierhuis. 2011. Beyond Cooperative Robotics: The Central Role of Interdependence in Coactive Design. *IEEE Intelligent Systems* 26 (3): 81–88.

Jourdan, D.B., et al. Enhancing UAV Survivability Through Damage Tolerant Control in Proceedings of the AIAA Guidance Navigation and Control Conference. 2010. AIAA.

Jurafsky, Daniel, James H. Martin. 2008. An Introduction to Natural Language Processing, Computational Linguistics, and Speech Recognition Second Edition.

Kaber, David B. and Mica R. Endsley. 1997. Out-of-the-Loop Performance Problems and the Use of Intermediate Levels of Automation for Improved Control System Functioning and Safety. *Process Safety Progress* 16 (3): 126-131.

Helmert, M.; Röger, G.; and Karpas, E. 2011. Fast Downward Stone Soup: A baseline for building planner portfolios. In Proceedings of the ICAPS-2011 Workshop on Planning and Learning (PAL), 28–35.

Klein, G.A., B. Moon, and R.R. Hoffman. 2006. Making Sense of Sensemaking 2: A Macrocognitive Model. *IEEE Intelligent Systems* 21 (6): 22–26.

Klein, Gary, et al. 2005. Problem Detection. *Cognition, Technology, and Work* 7 (1): 14–28.

Klein, Gary, et al. 2004. Ten Challenges for Making Automation a 'Team Player' in Joint Human-Agent Activity. *IEEE Intelligent Systems* 19 (6): 91–95.

Knox, Bradley, Peter Stone. 2011. Reinforcement Learning from Simultaneous Human and MDP Reward

Lee, John D. and Katrina A. See. 2004. Trust in Automation: Designing for Appropriate Reliance. *Human Factors* 46(1): 50-80.

Lucey, Danielle; "U.S. Officials Confirm Use of Sentinel in bin Laden Raid;" AUVSI Magazine, May 18, 2011.

McClurea, M., D.R. Corbettb, and D.W. Gage. The DARPA LANdroids program. in SPIE Unmanned Systems Technology XI,. 2009. SPIE.

McDermott, Drew, ed. 1998. The Planning Domain Definition Language Manual. Yale Computer Science Report 1165.

McGuirl, J.M., N.B. Sarter, and D.D. Woods. 2009. See is Believing? The Effects of Real-Time Imaging on Decision-Making in a Simulated Incident Command Task. *International Journal of Information Systems for Crisis Response and Management* 1 (1): 54–69.

Miller, C. and R. Parasuraman. 2007. Designing for Flexible Interaction Between Humans and Automation: Delegation Interfaces for Supervisory Control. *Human Factors* 49 (1): 57–75.

Morison A. and D.D. Woods. (in press). Human-Robot Interaction as Extended Perception. In *Cambridge Handbook of Applied Perception Research*, edited by R. R. Hoffman, P. A. Hancock, R. Parasuraman, J. L. Szalma, and M. Scerbo.

Morison, A., M. Voshell, A. Roesler, M. Feil, J. Tittle, D. Tinapple, and D.D. Woods. 2009. Integrating Diverse Feeds to Extend Human Perception into Distant Scenes. In *Advanced Decision Architectures for the Warfighter: Foundation and Technology,* edited by Patricia McDermott and Laurel Allander. Alion Science.

Mulder, M, J.J.A. Pauwelussen, M.M. Van Paassen, M. Mulder, and D.A. Abbink. 2010. Active Deceleration Support in Car Following. *IEEE Transactions on Systems, Man and Cybernetics—Part A: Systems and Humans* 40(6): 1271–1284.

Murphy, R.R. 2000. *Introduction to AI Robotics.* Cambridge, MA: MIT Press.

Murphy, R. R. and D.D. Woods. 2009. Beyond Asimov: The Three Laws of Responsible Robotics. *IEEE Intelligent Systems* 24(4): 14-20.

Murphy, R.R. and J.L. Burke. 2010. The Safe Human-Robot Ratio. In *Human-Robot Interactions in Future Military Operations*, edited by Michael Barnes and Florian Jentsch. 31-49. Burlington, VT: Ashgate.

Norman, D.A. 1990. The "Problem" with Automation: Inappropriate Feedback and Interaction, Not "Over-Automation". *Philosophical Transactions of the Royal Society of London* 327 (1241): 585–593.

Pan, S. J. and Yang, Q., 2008. "A survey on transfer learning."

Perry, S. J., R.L. Wear, and R.I. Cook. 2005. The Role of Automation in Complex System Failures. *Journal of Patient Safety* 1(1): 56-61.

Rogers, Everett M. 2003. *Diffusion of Innovations*. 5th edition. New York: Free Press.

Sarter, N.B. 2005. Graded and multimodal interruption cueing in support of pre-attentive reference and attention management. Proceedings of the Human Factors and Ergonomics Society 49th annual meeting. Santa Monica, CA: Human Factors and Ergonomics Society, 478–481.

Sarter, N.B. 2002. Multimodal Information Presentation in Support of Human Automation Communication and Coordination. In *Advances in Human Performance and Cognitive Engineering Research*, edited by E. Salas. 13-36. New York: JAI Press.

Sarter, N.B. and D.D. Woods. 1995. 'How in the World Did We Ever Get into that Mode?' Mode Error and Awareness in Supervisory Control. *Human Factors* 37 (1): 5-19.

Sarter, N.B., D.D. Woods, and C. Billings. 1997. Automation Surprises. In *Handbook of Human Factors/Ergonomics*, edited by Gavriel Salvendy. 2nd edition. 1926-1943. New York: Wiley. [Reprinted in N. Moray, ed. 2005. *Ergonomics: Major Writings*. New York: Taylor & Francis.]

Savage-Knepshield, Pamela, ed. 2012. *Designing Soldier Systems: Current Issues in Human Factors*. Burlington, VT: Ashgate.

Sebe, Nicu, Ira Cohen, Ashutosh Garg, and Thomas S. Huang. 2005. *Machine Learning in Computer Vision*. Dordrecht: Springer.

Settles, Burr. 2011. Closing the Loop: Fast, Interactive Semi-Supervised Annotation with Queries on Features and Instances. *EMNLP '11 Proceedings of the Conference on Empirical Methods in Natural Language Processing*: 1467-1478.

Shattuck, L.G. and D. D. Woods. 2000. Communication of Intent in Military Command and Control Systems. In *The Human in Command: Exploring the Modern Military Experience*, edited by Carol McCann and Ross Pigeau. 279-292. New York: Kluwer Academic/Plenum Publishers.

Sheridan, Thomas B. 1992. *Telerobotics, Automation, and Human Supervisory Control*. Cambridge, MA: MIT Press.

Simon, Herbert A. 1996. *The Sciences of the Artificial*. 3rd edition. Cambridge, MA: MIT Press.

Sklar, A.E. and N.B. Sarter. 1999. 'Good Vibrations': the Use of Tactile Feedback in Support of Mode Awareness on Advanced Technology Aircraft. *Human Factors* 41 (4): 543–552.

Smith, P.J., C.E. McCoy, and C. Layton. 1997. Brittleness in the Design of Cooperative Problem-Solving Systems: The Effects on User Performance. *IEEE Transactions on Systems, Man, and Cybernetics* 27 (3): 360-371.

Sutton, Richard S. 1998. *Reinforcement Learning*. Cambridge, MA: MIT Press.

Technology Horizons, Volume 1; AF/ST-TR-10-01; 15 May 2010

Trafton, J. Gregory, et al. 2005. Enabling Effective Human-Robot Interaction Using Perspective-Taking in Robots. *IEEE Transactions on Systems, Man, and Cybernetics—Part A: Systems and Humans* 35 (4): 460–470.

U.S. Department of Defense. 2009. FY2009-2034 Unmanned Systems Integrated Roadmap. Washington, DC: U.S. Department of Defense.

U.S. Department of Defense. 2011. National Space Strategy. Washington, DC: U.S. Department of Defense.

U.S. Department of Defense. 2009. Policies and Procedures for the Acquisition of Information Technology. Washington, DC: U.S. Department of Defense.

U.S. Government Accountability Office. 2005. New DoD Space Science and Technology Strategy Provides Basis for Optimizing Investments, but Future Versions Need to Be More Robust. Washington, DC: U.S. Government Accountability Office.

U.S. Navy. 2007. Unmanned Surface Vehicle Master Plan.

U.S. Navy. 2004. Unmanned Undersea Vehicle (UUV) Master Plan.

Watts-Perotti J. and D.D. Woods. 2009. Cooperative Advocacy: A Strategy for Integrating Diverse Perspectives in Anomaly Response. *Computer Supported Cooperative Work: The Journal of Collaborative Computing* 18 (2): 175–198.

Wiener, Earl L., and Renwick E. Curry. 1980. Flight-deck Automation: Promises and Problems. *Ergonomics* 23 (10): 995–1011.

Wiese, E.E. and J.D. Lee. 2007. Attention Grounding: A New Approach to In-Vehicle Information System Implementation. *Theoretical Issues in Ergonomics Science* 8 (3): 255–276.

Winograd, T. and D.D. Woods. 1997. Challenges for Human-Centered Design. In *Human-Centered Systems: Information, Interactivity, and Intelligence*, edited by J. Flanagan, et al. Washington, DC: National Science Foundation.

Woods, D.D. and E. Hollnagel. 2006. *Joint Cognitive Systems: Patterns in Cognitive Systems Engineering.* Boca Raton, FL: Taylor & Francis.

Woods, D.D., E.S. Patterson, and E.M. Roth. 2002. Can We Ever Escape from Data Overload? A Cognitive Systems Diagnosis. *Cognition, Technology, and Work* 4 (1): 22–36.

Woods, D. D. and M. Branlat. 2010. Hollnagel's Test: Being 'In Control' of Highly Interdependent Multi-layered Networked Systems. *Cognition, Technology, and Work* 12(2): 95-101.

Woods, D. D. and N.B. Sarte. 2010. Capturing the Dynamics of Attention Control from Individual to Distributed Systems. *Theoretical Issues in Ergonomics* 11(1): 7-28.

Woods, D.D. and N.B. Sarter. 2000. Learning from Automation Surprises and Going Sour Accidents. In *Cognitive Engineering in the Aviation Domain*, edited by N. Sarter and R. Amalberti. 327-354. Hillsdale, NJ: Erlbaum.

Woods, D.D., S.W.A. Dekker, R.I. Cook, L.L. Johannesen, and N.B. Sarter. 2010. *Behind Human Error*. 2nd edition. Burlington, VT: Ashgate.

Younes, Hakan L.S. and Michael L. Littmann. 2004. PPDDL 1.0: An Extension to PDDL for Expressing Planning Domains with Probabilistic Effects. Carnegie Mellon University, School of Computer Science. http://reports-archive.adm.cs.cmu.edu/anon/anon/home/ftp/2004/CMU-CS-04-167.pdf.

Zieba, S., P. Polet, and F. Vanderhaegen. 2011. Using Adjustable Autonomy and Human–Machine Cooperation to Make a Human–Machine System Resilient-Application to a Ground Robotic System. *Information Sciences* 181(3): 379–397.

Appendix C—Task Force Terms of Reference

THE UNDER SECRETARY OF DEFENSE
3010 DEFENSE PENTAGON
WASHINGTON, DC 20301-3010

ACQUISITION,
TECHNOLOGY
AND LOGISTICS

MEMORANDUM FOR CHAIRMAN, DEFENSE SCIENCE BOARD

SUBJECT: Terms of Reference - Defense Science Board Task Force on the Role of
Autonomy in Department of Defense (DoD) Systems

Dramatic progress in supporting technologies suggests that unprecedented, perhaps unimagined, degrees of autonomy can be introduced into current and future military systems. This could presage dramatic changes in military capability and force composition comparable to the introduction of "Net-Centricity." It is important that DoD understand and prepare to take maximum practical advantage of advances in this area. The timing is especially important as we introduce significant numbers of unmanned systems into the force and perhaps limit their capability by imposing restraints associated with manned concepts upon the capabilities of new systems.

You are requested to form a Task Force that will inform the Department's plans in this area; specifically, the Task Force should:

- Review relevant technologies and ongoing research and development (R&D) of autonomous systems to evaluate the readiness of autonomous systems, or autonomy improvements, for introduction into DoD.

- Identify and review current plans of the Military Departments for the integration of autonomy in current or near-term systems and employment of next-generation autonomous systems and analyze missed opportunities.

- Assess the personnel training and force structure impacts of various improvements to autonomy, including opportunities, to reduce weapon system and associated personal forward footprint.

- Identify new opportunities for more aggressive application of autonomy to U.S. military materiel and the benefits this might provide to our military posture and the accomplishment of military missions.

- Comment upon the potential value of autonomy to both symmetric and asymmetric adversaries and, where possible, review available intelligence, and provide the basis for net assessment.

- Anticipate new vulnerabilities that deployment and battlefield reliance on large-scale, pervasive autonomous systems might introduce, especially those which could be gainfully exploited by an adversary. At the same time, be alert to the possibility that autonomy might hedge against weaknesses in net-centricity, which may result from network vulnerabilities.

- Identify systemic barriers to fully realizing the potential of autonomous systems including failures of imagination and constraints of current doctrine, self-imposed handicaps imposed by applying manned concepts to new systems, lack of an informed, motivated industrial base, and DoD's current acquisition processes.

- Identify special needs in testing and in modeling and simulation to assist in evaluation of specific autonomous enablers and associated concepts of operation.

- Review operational difficulties in rapid introduction of such capabilities, including: workforce composition, personnel skills and training, systems reliability and sustainability, asserted incompatibilities with legacy and currently planned systems, safety regulation for operation in civilian spaces and transportation lanes, and the impact of regulations on R&D in the United States.

The Task Force should deliver a roadmap for realizing as rapidly and efficiently as possible the battlefield potential of autonomous systems.

The study will be sponsored by the Under Secretary of Defense for Acquisition, Technology and Logistics. Dr Robin Murphy and Mr. James Shields will co-chair the Task Force. Mr. James M. Durham and Commander Dylan Schmorrow, USN, of ODDR&E will serve as Executive Secretaries, and Lieutenant Colonel Karen Walters, USA, will serve as the DSB Secretariat Representative.

The Task Force will operate in accordance with the provisions of P.L. 92-463, the "Federal Advisory Committee Act," and DoD Directive 5105.4, the "DoD Federal Advisory Committee Management Program." It is not anticipated that this Task Force will need to go into any "particular matters" within the meaning of title 18, U.S. Code, section 208, nor will it cause any member to be placed in the position of acting as a procurement official.

PDUSD(ACT)

Ashton B. Carter

2

Appendix D—Task Force Membership

Co-Chairs

Dr. Robin Murphy	Texas A&M University
Mr. James Shields	Charles Stark Draper Laboratory

Executive Secretary

CAPT Dylan Schmorrow	ASD(R&E)

Members

Dr. Brent Appleby	DARPA
Dr. Adele Howe	Colorado State University
Maj. Gen. Ken Israel, USAF (Ret.)	Lockheed Martin, Co.
Dr. Alexis Livanos	Northrop Grumman Corporation
Gen. James McCarthy, USAF (Ret.)	USAF Academy
Dr. Raymond Mooney	University of Texas-Austin
ADM John Nathman, USN (Ret.)	Independent Consultant
Dr. Kevin Parker	Harvard University
Dr. Robert Tenney	BAE Systems
Dr. David Woods	Ohio State University

Senior Advisors

Dr. John Foster	Northrop Grumman
Dr. Anita Jones	University of Virginia

DSB Secretariat

Mr. Brian Hughes	DSB Executive Director
CDR Robert Medve, USN	DSB Military Assistant
CDR Douglas Reinbold, USN	DSB Military Assistant

Support

Mr. Christopher Grisafe	SAIC
Ms. Tammy-Jean Beatty	SAIC
Mr. Jason Wood	SAIC

Appendix E—Task Force Briefings

Briefing Title	Briefer	Organization
Air Force ISR	Brig. Gen. Robert Otto	USAF HQ
Science of Autonomy	Dr. Marc Steinberg	ONR
Artificial Intelligence	Dr. Allan Schultz	NRL
Autonomy for Marine Vehicles	Mr. Steve Castelin	USN
Removing Systemic Barriers to Autonomous Systems	Mr. John Lambert	AUVSI
USAF SAB Outbrief and Perspective on Autonomy	Mr. Greg Zacharias	SAB
Unmanned Ground Vehicle Roadmap	Mr. Patrick Cantwell	USMC
Army Capabilities	LTC Stu Hatfield	USA
OUSD (AT&L) Unmanned Systems Program Overview	Mr. Dyke Weatherington	OSD
AF Unmanned Aircraft Systems Flight Plan, 2009-2047	Lt. Gen. Dave Deptula	USAF
UAV/UAV 25 Year Roadmap	COL John Lynch	USA Center of Excellence
Ground-Based Sense-See-and-Avoid Efforts	COL Gregory Gonzales	USA
DARPA Programs	Dr. Robbie Mandelbaum	Private Consultant
Strategic Future of Autonomy in the Air Force	Dr. J.A. Dahm	USAF
Northrop Grumman	Dr. Michael Leahy	Northrop Grumman
General Atomics Aeronautics	Jeff Hettick	General Atomics
Lockheed Martin	Mr. Neil Kacena	Lockheed Martin
Boeing	Dr. Randall Rothe	Boeing
QinetiQ	Dr. Scott Thayer	QinetiQ
General Dynamics	Mr. Phil Cory	General Dynamics
Joint Unmanned Aircraft Systems Center of Excellence JUAV COE	Staff	JUAV COE
Remotely Piloted Aircraft Mission Brief	Brig Gen (Sel.) Peter Gersten	Creech AFB
Musings on Autonomy	Dr. Gill Pratt	DARPA
NUWC Division Newport State of Autonomy for Unmanned Undersea Vehicles	Mr. James Griffin	NUWC

Appendix F—Glossary

4D/RCS	Real-time Control System
A2AD	Anti Access Area Denial
ADCR	Automatically Deployed Communication Relays
ADEPT	All-Domain Execution and Planning Technology
ADUUV	Advanced Development Unmanned Undersea Vehicle
AEODRS	Advanced Explosive Ordnance Disposal Robotic Systems
AFB	Air Force Base
AFSPC	Air Force Space Command
AI	Artificial Intelligence
AOR	Area of Responsibility
ARCI/APB	Advanced Rapid COTS [Commercial Off The Shelf] Insertion/Advanced Processor Build
ARGOS	On-time information system
ARM	Autonomous Robotic Manipulation
ASD(R&E)	Assistant Secretary of Defense for Research and Engineering
ASR	Automated Speech Recognition
ASTM	American Society for Testing and Materials
ASW	Ant-Submarine Warfare
ATC	Air Traffic Controller
AUSV	Autonomous Unmanned Surface Vehicle
BAMS	Broad Area Maritime Surveillance
BPAUV	Battlespace Preparation Autonomous Underwater Vehicle
C2	Command and Control
C4ISR	Command, Control, Communications, Computers, Intelligence, Surveillance and Reconnaissance
C-IED	Counter Improvised Explosive Device
CA	Counter-Autonomy
CALO	Cognitive Assistant that Learns to Organize
CAP	Combat Air Patrol
CAOC	Combined Air Operation Center
CASPER	Continuous Activity Scheduling Planning Execution and Replanning
CBRN	Chemical, Biological, Radiological, and Nuclear
CBRNE	Chemical, Biological, Radiological, Nuclear or High-yield Explosive
CNAV	Collaborative Networked Autonomous Vehicle
CNO	Chief of Naval Operations
COI	Community of Interest
COIN	Counterinsurgency
CONOPS	Concept of Operations

CONUS	Continental United States
COTS	Commercial off the Shelf
CPD	Capability Production Documents
CSCI	Computer Software Configuration Item
CSG	Carrier Strike Group
DARPA	Defense Advanced Research Projects Agency
DASN (C4I)	Deputy Assistant Secretary of the Navy – C4I
DCGS	Distributed Common Ground Station
DDS	Dry Deck Shelter
DIA	Defense Intelligence Agency
DoD	Department of Defense
DOE	Department of Energy
DSB	Defense Science Board
EDM	Engineering Development Model
EO	Electro-Optic
EOD	Explosive Ordnance Disposal
ETMS	Engineering Works & Traffic Information Management System
FMV	Full Motion Video
FYDP	Future Year Defense Program
FYDPEDM	Future Years Defense Plan Engineering Development Model
GCS	Ground Control Station
GIG	Global Information Grid
GIGFYDP	Global Information Grid Future Years Defense Plan
GMTI	Ground Moving Target Indicator
GN&C	Guidance, Navigation and Control
GPS	Global Positioning System
GUI	Graphical User Interface
GWOT	Global War on Terror
HRI	Human-robot Interaction
HVT	High Value Target
I&WGIG	Indications and Warnings Global Information Grid
ICAO	International Civil Aviation Organization
IED	Improvised Explosive Device
IEEE	Institute of Electrical and Electronics Engineers
INP	Innovative Naval Prototype
IOC	Information Operations Center
IOCI&W	Initial Operational Capability Indications and Warnings
IOE	Integrated Operations Environment
ISCA	Integrated Sensor Coverage Area
ISR	Intelligence, Reconnaissance and Surveillance
ISRIOCGIG	Intelligence, Reconnaissance and Surveillance Initial Operational Capability

	Global Information Grid
IT	Information Technology
JIATF-S	Joint Inter-Agency Task Force-South
JIATF-SI&W	Joint Inter Agency Task Force – South Indications and Warnings
JPL	Jet Propulsion Laboratory
JROC	Joint Requirements Oversight Council
LADAR	Laser Radar
LAGR	Learning Applied to Ground Robotics
LCS	Littoral Combat Ship
LCSJIATF-SIOC	Littoral Combat Ship Joint Inter Agency Task Force – South Initial Operational Capability
LDUUV	Large Displacement Unmanned Undersea Vehicle
LDUUVLCS	Large Displacement Unmanned Undersea Vehicle Littoral Combat Ship
LIA	Logistics Innovation Agency
LIDAR	Light Detection and Ranging
LMCLDUUVJIATF-S	Lockheed Martin Corp Large Displacement Unmanned Undersea Vehicle Joint Inter Agency Task Force - South
LMRS	Long-Term Mine Reconnaissance System
LMRSLMCLCS	Long Term Mine Reconnaissance System Lockheed Martin Corp Littoral Combat Ship
MANPADS	Man-Portable Air-Defense Systems
MCM	Mine Counter Measure
MCMMOSALMC	Mine Counter Measure Modular Open-Systems Approach Lockheed Martin Corp
MISUS	Multi-Rover Integrated Science Understanding System
MOAA	Maritime Open Architecture Autonomy
MOCU	Multi-Robot Operator Control Unit
MOSA	Modular Open-Systems Approach
MOSALMRSLDUUV	Modular Open-Systems Approach Long Term Mine Reconnaissance System Large Displacement Unmanned Undersea Vehicle
MRAP	Mine Resistant Ambush Protected
MRUUVS	Mission Reconfigurable Unmanned Undersea Vehicle System
MS-BMCMLMRS	Milestone BMine Counter Measure Long Term Mine Reconnaissance System
MSDF	Maritime Self Defense Force
MUM	Manned-Unmanned
NASA	National Aeronautics and Space Administration
NCO	Non-Commissioned Officer
NGA	National Geospatial Intelligence Agency
NIST	National Institute of Standards and Technology
NIWO	Navy Irregular Warfare Office
NLP	Natural Language Processing
NLU	Natural Language Understanding

NMRS	Near-Term Mine Reconnaissance System
NOAA	National Oceanic and Atmospheric Administration
NRL	Naval Research Laboratory
NRT	Near Real Time
OA	Open Architecture
OCS	Operator Control System
OCSMS-BMOSA	Milestone BModular Open-Systems Approach
OCU	Operator Control Unit
OGO	Other Government Organization
ONR	Office of Naval Research
ONRMCM	Office of Naval Research (Mine Counter Measure
OOTL	Out-of-the-loop
OPTEVAL	Operational Test and Evaluation
OPTEVALONRMS-B	Operational Test and Evaluation Office of Naval Research (Milestone B
OSD	Office of the Secretary of Defense
OT&E	Operational, Test and Evaluation
PDDL	Planning Domain Definition Language
PEO	Program Executive Office
PLUS	Persistent Littoral Undersea Surveillance
POR	Program of Record
R&D	Research and Development
RDT&E	Research, Development, Test and Evaluation
REMUS	Remote Environmental Monitoring Unit System
RF	Radiofrequency
RGB-R	Red, Green, Blue
RHIB	Rigid-hulled inflatable boat
RMS	Remote Minehunting System
ROE	Rules of Engagement
RSO	Remote-Split Operations
RSTA	Reconnaissance, Surveillance and Target Acquisition
RT	Real Time
S&T	Science and Technology
SDR	Software for Distributed Robots
SET	Satellite Enterprise Transformation
SIGINT	Signals Intelligence
SLOC	Software Lines of Code
SMC	Space and Missile Systems Center
SMCM	Surface Mine Countermeasure
SOA	Service Oriented Architecture

SPAWAR	Space and Naval Warfare Systems Command
SPIN	Special Instruction
SSGN	Guided-Missile Submarine
SSKSSGN	Diesel Submarine Guided-Missile Submarine
SSN	Attack submarine
SSNSSK	Fast Attack Submarine Diesel Submarine
SUBFORS&TSSN	Submarine Force Science and Technology Fast Attack Submarine
SUBFORSUBFOR	Submarine Force Submarine Force
SUT	System Under Test
T&E	Test and Evaluation
T-REX	Teleo-Reactive-Executive
TSPI	Time-Space-Position-Information
TOW	Tube-launched, Optically-tracked, Wire Command
TTPT&E	Tactics, Techniques, and Procedures Test and Evaluation
UAV	Unmanned Aerial Vehicle
UCAV	Unmanned Combat Aircraft Vehicle
UCI	Unmanned Aerial Vehicle Command and Control Initiative
UGV	Unmanned Ground Systems
UHF	Ultra-High Frequency
UMV	Unmanned Maritime Vehicle
UMVTTPT&E	Unmanned Maritime Vehicle Tactics, Techniques, and Procedures Test and Evaluation
UPI	Off-Road Autonomy
USD(AT&L)	Under Secretary of Defense for Acquisition, Technology and Logistics
USD(AT&L) UMVTTP	Under Secretary of Defense for Acquisition, Technology and Logistics Unmanned Maritime Vehicle Tactics, Techniques, and Procedures
USAF	United States Air Force
USV	Unmanned Surface Vehicle
UUV	Unmanned Undersea Vehicle
UUVUMV	Unmanned Undersea Vehicle Unmanned Maritime Vehicle
UxV	Unmanned Vehicle
V&V	Verification and Validation
VIRAT	Video and Image Retrieval and Analysis Tool